THE
TRAILRIDER GUIDE

SPAIN

REVOLUTION PUBLISHING

Life in Cycles

Mountain bike. n. A bicycle with a light
sturdy frame, broad deep-treaded tyres,
and multiple gears, originally designed
for riding on mountainous terrain.
(Concise Oxford Dictionary, tenth edition.)

THE TRAILRIDER GUIDE SPAIN

REVOLUTION PUBLISHING
www.revolutionpublishing.com
www.trailriderguide.com

First published in 2004 by
REVOLUTION PUBLISHING

Creation of all maps, graphics,
graphs, text and photographs
REVOLUTION PUBLISHING ©

ISBN reference: 0-9547904-0-5

Printed in the UK by
Stephens and George Ltd.

THE
TRAILRIDER
GUIDE

SPAIN

Whilst we try to provide something for everyone, the rides are aimed most specifically at cross country/free-riders. This book is therefore aimed at those who have ability and like technical, challenging riding.

JAMES NATHAN
Publisher/ Editor/ Rider/
Photographer

LINSEY STROUD
Editor/ Graphics & Design/
Photographer/ Researcher

Technical support:
Steve Herring,
Dan Haylock - Low Pressure
Publications

Moral support:
Our Parents, Rob and Talia
Findlay, Mud Dock Bristol,
Dave Madden, Robert Aplin,
Ollie Fitzjones, Simon Beatson,
Pete Abram, All at El Berro
Camping, Michael at Bike
Station Marbella, Michael from
Switchbacks.com, Molly and
Tony, Clive Ripley, Amanda and
Gareth Rowe, Jo Olivier, All at
Cube Nu-Media, Cesar and the
Arenas de San Pedro equipo, Kit
and Juanjo, Anna and Fifi,
Martin and Camilla Darburn,
the bee man from Camping San
Isico, The Neurekers, Alistair
Sawday, Brian at Trek, Rupert
Wheeler, Pippa Williscroft, our
nanas, Helen Franklin.

FOREWORD

When I decided to take a year off and go mountain biking around Europe I thought it would be simple. I decided to compile a list of the best destinations to visit and then spend months cycling the best dry trails on the Continent.

To create a list I talked to my local bike shop. To my surprise they could tell me very little. I was met with scratched heads and a couple of rumours about "Sierral Nevadal" being quite good (I'm from Bristol mind!) but little else. With my short list of one I turned to guidebooks but was disappointed to find seriously out of date and tedious riding itineraries.

I continued my research on the Internet. Obviously lists of places promising good riding appeared at my first click and I thought my search was at an end. However, when I scratched below the surface I was dismayed to find an incredible lack of detail. Although I found out where there were good riding 'resorts' there was no specific details of legendary trails.

I started questioning people who had actually visited these sumptuous riding destinations and from those discussions came the motivation for this book.

I discovered that countless riders return from superb mountain biking venues frustrated at not being able to find even a sniff of decent singletrack.

It became glaringly obvious what I needed to do. I sold my house, gathered my girlfriend, a bike, camera and a Land Rover and set off to the best biking destination in Europe to compile a list of these secret trails.

We were looking for the kind of endless ribbons of trail that you wouldn't have found without a local's help. We immersed ourselves in the heart of the Spanish countryside and learnt to speak some very dodgy local dialects so we could ride with mental locals to find some intense routes.

Having spent a year riding and having added over ½ stone (sorry 6 kg's) of muscle to my legs, I am pleased to present you with the fruits of our labour. What follows is a guide to some of the best destinations in Spain. We have ridden every route, taken every photo and written every word to deliver a local rider's perspective of contemporary trail riding in Spain.

SPAIN

Spain is one of the most mountainous countries in Europe. This huge landmass has a surprisingly small population and consequently there are hoards of virgin trails waiting to be discovered. The sheer size and number of mountain ranges means there is practically every type of terrain imaginable; something for every riding taste. Rural tourism is on the increase and old rights of way are being rediscovered and reopened. These ancient cattle trails and trading routes make excellent riding. Add to these routes some of Europe's best weather conditions and you have all the right ingredients to make this a mountain biking heaven. In particular, the southern province of Andalucia has been dubbed the 'California of Europe' and dry riding is commonplace when all other European destinations are washed out.

Whatever you are looking for, SPAIN has it for you.

THE

TRAILRIDER
GUIDE

S P A I N

CONTENTS

Introduction

Northern Spain

Central Spain

Eastern Spain

Southern Spain

MOUNTAIN SAFETY

WARNING

Mountain biking is an inherently dangerous activity that you undertake at your own risk. Our routes explore the most technically demanding singletrack we could find so, by definition, they are dangerous. These routes explore remote mountainous regions and you must be properly prepared for the conditions. Only attempt a ride if you have a reasonable degree of fitness and good quality equipment. *A cheap cycle will* NOT *survive these rigorous routes.*

We hope we have done all we can to help you find and ride the most obscure and inspiring routes in Spain. If you lose your way or can't decipher our instructions, try to remember through your wrath that, without the book, you wouldn't have known some of these places even existed let alone where to look for the local trails.

BASIC SAFETY

Having enough water is essential. Springs and streams in the UK are usually undrinkable but in Spain most springs are safe to drink from unless they say 'agua non potable' ('not drinking water'). Always try to be self-sufficient and carry enough water for your route and use springs as a back-up should you run low. 'Fuente' and 'manantial' are Spanish words for 'spring' and usually indicate a place where drinking water can be found.

Many rides take a day to complete but breakdowns, injuries, bad weather, getting lost and unforeseen circumstances can cause you to be out for longer than planned. Go prepared for such eventualities. **You should never ride alone.** Always plot your progress on a map. Always let someone know where you are going, the route you are taking, when you expect to return and what to do if you don't. Leave all valuables locked in the boot of your car or out of site before you park up and don't leave messages that would be of interest to thieves. Check weather forecasts and know what happens to the local temperature when the sun goes down. Have suitable clothing for the conditions.

Check your bike before each ride particularly tyre pressures, wheel, steering and brake integrity. The more often you do this the easier it is to spot problems. You must be able to perform basic trailside repairs. Always carry your own repair kit so that you are self sufficient if separated from the group. Multi-tools allow you to carry a great deal of equipment compactly. Keep your repair kit serviced; finding perished inner tubes and dried out patch kit when you need them most can be distressing. In addition to tools, you need to carry basic safety equipment. Always wear a helmet and carry a lightweight, weatherproof jacket. Take sufficient water, a high-energy snack and map, mobile phone, money/credit-card, sunscreen, torch/candle and a first aid kit.

TRAIL SENSE

INFECTION

If you graze or cut yourself in areas where there are goats you should disinfect the wound as soon as possible. These animals carry a microbe that can infect wounds and even a small graze can become a potentially serious injury requiring significant treatment. Disinfecting a wound with TCP or iodine can prevent this.

BODY PROTECTION

It can be worth strapping lightweight elbow and shin pads to your trail pack. Keep them there whilst ascending to avoid hot and sticky skin but put them on for long descents. They can protect you from tough undergrowth as you whiz by and rocks being thrown up. Many descents are longer, drier and rockier than you may be used to increasing the likelihood of a spill; padding will help protect you.

OTHER PEOPLE

Always ride in control and approach others courteously. Greet hikers well in advance in a normal voice when approaching from behind. It is particularly easy for bikers to startle horses because they do not hear your approach. Make your presence known well in advance. Remember that mountain bikers can look like they are on their way to some kind of futuristic space battle and your appearance may intimidate others. Put them at their ease. Smile.

OTHER BIKERS

Don't ride more than two abreast on roads and at least three bike lengths apart on singletrack. Maintain a minimum of ten bike lengths apart on all descents. Each rider should maintain contact with the rider behind him, and, should a rider become separated, the group should return to the place of last contact. Make sure you agree that you will all do this to avoid confusion.

TRAIL WELFARE

Think about the trail surface. Try and develop clean smooth riding styles that don't damage trail surfaces. If you find obstructions or damage to a trail try to mend it. If you fall off and cause damage, repair it. Don't cut across switchbacks or create new paths. Respect closed routes and don't ride on private land. Get passes and/or permission from appropriate authorities where necessary.

MOUNTAIN ILLNESS

HEAT EXHAUSTION & HEAT STROKE

Your body cools down by sweating and increasing blood flow to the skin. Obviously this is harder to do when mountain biking in a hot country like Spain and there is a danger of overheating.

1. HEAT EXHAUSTION.

Heat exhaustion starts when, in its attempt to stay cool, the body has sent too much blood into the skin. This causes a loss of circulating blood volume, which decreases the blood supply to the brain and can cause fainting, weakness and nausea. Getting out of the sun, resting and having cold water will usually revive the afflicted.

Symptoms: disorientation, fainting, nausea, dizziness, weakness, headaches or heavy perspiration. The pulse may be weak and pupils dilated.

Treatment: remove yourself from sun, lie down, drink plenty of fluids and fan to cool.

2. HEAT STROKE.

Heat stroke is far more serious. It occurs when your body becomes so hot that it cannot cool down by itself and needs external help. You can be particularly vulnerable when you stop riding because you no longer creating airflow across the skin which can aid cooling. Heat stroke can therefore occur when you end a ride. It is a dangerous condition, effectively being the reverse of hypothermia. Seek medical attention immediately.

Symptoms from mild to severe: headache, nausea, and dizziness. Red, dry, very hot skin (sweating has ceased), pulse strong and rapid, small pupils, very high fever, may become extremely disoriented, unconsciousness and possible convulsions.

Treatment: remove victim to cooler location, out of the sun. Loosen or remove clothing and immerse victim in very cool water (e.g. a stream) if possible. If immersion isn't possible, cool victim with water, or wrap in wet sheets and fan for quick evaporation. It is not advisable to give the victim anything by mouth (even water) until the condition has been stabilised.

 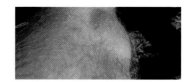

MOUNTAIN ILLNESS

HYPOTHERMIA

Hypothermia is suffered when the core body temperature drops below 35°C i.e. below normal functioning temperature of 37°C. Treating hypothermia is extremely difficult and can kill if done incorrectly. The treatment you give depends on the severity of symptoms. Always seek medical attention even if patient seems to recover.

Symptoms : Initial: shivering and fatigue. Mild: uncontrolled, intense shivering and loss of co-ordination. Cold causing pain. Moderate: shivering slows, muscles stiffen. Mental confusion. Speech vague/slurred. Breathing slower. Drowsy. Severe: weak, lack of co-ordination and appears drunk. Gradual loss of consciousness. Little or no apparent breathing, victim may be very rigid, unconscious, and may appear dead.

Treatment: Instinctively you would warm someone by covering them with blankets and sitting them by a fire. With hypothermia this course of action can kill them. You have to leave the extremities cold and warm the core first. The patient must be handled gently and not allowed to exercise, as muscular action can shunt cold blood from the extremities into the warmer core causing possible heart failure. For initial and mild hypothermia remove from cold, insulate and provide hot sweet drink and high-energy food. For moderate to severe cases shelter from the cold and wet, use shared body heat with the aim of stopping temperature drop, NOT re-warming. Introduce warm breath/steam to the patient's mouth area.

N.B. Cold can protect vital systems. A Patient may appear dead but never assume this until warm and dead!

ALTITUDE SICKNESS

Oxygen levels decrease the higher you climb from sea level so your body has to work harder to perform basic tasks, harder still if you are exercising. Altitude sickness is your body's reaction to the lack of oxygen. It usually occurs at elevations above 2,500 metres. It is a lottery who suffers but the basic cause is usually going up too high too fast. Acclimatisation is the key to avoidance. Try to stay somewhere on the way up. Sleep lower than you spend the day so you allow your body to adjust overnight. Make sure everyone in the group has acclimatised. Pay particular attention to hydration as you experience greater fluid loss at higher altitudes but may not feel as thirsty.
Keep activity light until you have properly adjusted.
Avoid alcohol and tobacco. Eat lots of carbohydrates.

Symptoms from mild to severe: headache, light-headedness, weakness, trouble sleeping and upset stomach. Difficulty breathing even when resting, coughing, confusion and inability to walk straight.

Treatment: go down to lower altitudes until symptoms cease. If severe seek medical attention.

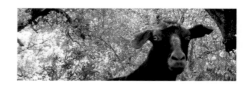

TRAIL CRITTERS

BEE, WASP AND HORNET STINGS

Found in hollow trees, caves, swimming pools and dwellings, you will come across wasps and bees all over Spain. If stung by a bee, immediately remove the stinger and venom sac, if attached, by scraping with a fingernail or a knife blade. Do not squeeze or grasp the stinger or venom sac, as squeezing will force more venom into the wound. Wash the sting site thoroughly with soap and water to lessen the chance of a secondary infection.

Relieve the itching and discomfort caused by insect bites by applying:
cold compresses;
a cooling paste of mud and ashes;
sap from dandelions;
coconut meat;
crushed cloves of garlic;
onion.

SCORPION STINGS

You can come across scorpions in Spain, particularly at night. Scorpions are all poisonous to a greater or lesser degree but, as a general rule, the more translucent the body the more venomous the creature. They like living in decaying matter, under debris, logs and rocks and like to hide in boots. Treat scorpion stings by cleaning and dressing the bite area to reduce the risk of infection. The sting will hurt but death is rare, occurring mainly in children or adults with high blood pressure or illnesses.

SNAKE BITES

Snakes live in crevices of rocks, walls and trees. Bites can occur when people rest on rocky piles or walls disturbing the snake. They have a tendency to aim for dark places so beware that a trouser leg or baggy short is an inviting bolt hole. Deaths from snakebites are rare but shock and panic can affect recovery. Excitement, hysteria, and panic can speed up the circulation causing the body to absorb the toxin quickly. If you know that a poisonous snake has bitten an individual, take the following steps:

reassure the victim and keep him/her still;
remove watches, rings, bracelets or other constricting items;
clean the bite area;
maintain an airway (especially if bitten near the face or neck);
use a constricting band between the wound and the heart;
immobilise the site;
remove the poison as soon as possible by using a mechanical suction device or by squeezing.

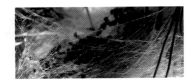

TRAIL CRITTERS

Do not:
give the victim alcoholic beverages or tobacco products;
give morphine or other central nervous system depressants;
make any deep cuts at the bite site. Cutting opens capillaries that in turn
open a direct route into the blood stream for venom and infection.

A bite wound, regardless of the type of animal that inflicted it, can become infected
from bacteria in the animal's mouth. With non-poisonous as well as poisonous snake
bites this local infection is responsible for a large part of the residual damage that results.

TICKS

Ticks can carry and transmit diseases including Lyme disease. If you find ticks attached to your body cover
them with a substance such as Vaseline, heavy oil or tree sap that will cut off their air supply. Without air
the tick releases its hold and you can remove it. Take care to remove the whole tick. Use tweezers if you
have them. Grasp the tick where the mouth-parts are attached to the skin. Do not squeeze the body as this
can inject infection into your blood stream. Wash your hands after
touching the tick and clean the wound daily until healed.

TARANTULAS

Tarantulas are found in parts of Andalucia. They live in dark, cool, damp
places such as under rocks. Their large fangs inflict painful bites but it is
rare to see them. Treat as with other bites and seek medical attention.

CENTIPEDES

These multi-jointed creatures can give a surprisingly painful bite. Their
bright red and yellow colourings warn you of their dangers. They live
under bark and stones by day and are active at night.

PROCESSIONAL CATERPILLARS

The pine processionary moth (Thaumetopoea pityocampa) is a serious
pest in pine forests and is found all over Spain, particularly in
plantations. They migrate by attaching themselves to others and forming
long snake-like processions (hence the name). You will see their
web-like nests high up in pine trees. The caterpillars of the moth have
irritant hairs that cause severe itching and allergic reaction. Watch out
for them in sleeping bags. Don't touch the nests or the caterpillars.

BODY REPAIR

ELECTROLYTES

Electrolytes are important salts and minerals necessary for essential bodily functions such as transmitting nerve impulses, regulating fluid and chemical levels and they are an integral part of the sweating process. Given the number of important jobs they perform it is important to replace them. Sports drinks manufacturers capitalise on this idea but in truth it isn't really possible to replace them as you use them on a ride. They are most effectively recovered from fresh fruit and vegetables at the end of your ride. Sports drinks can help replace certain things but can never substitute a healthy diet. Everyone has a unique electrolytic pattern so there is no ideal dosage. They are useful in small quantities but if too concentrated they inhibit the absorption of fluid into the body. Some theories say the absence of these elements causes cramp.

ELECTROLYTES AND CRAMP

A cramp occurs when a muscle tightens and shortens causing a sudden severe pain. Although it is clear what a cramp is, there is no clear understanding of why they occur. The two most popular theories blame dehydration and electrolyte imbalance. The Dehydration Theory says that water loss means your blood volume is lower so there is less blood going to muscles to deliver oxygen, resulting in a muscle spasm. The Electrolyte Imbalance Theory says because electrolytes regulate nerve impulses and muscle

contraction, if you lose sufficient electrolytes your body loses the ability to control muscle contractions and they contract involuntarily causing a cramp. Regardless of which theory is correct, fluid consumption seems an important way of minimising the risk of cramp. Treat cramp by relaxing the tightened area and gently massaging it. Try to stretch the muscle out slowly and gently.

BODY REPAIR

HYDRATION

When riding in the heat dehydration is a serious problem as it can impair both physical and mental performance. By the time you are thirsty, you may already be 2 - 3% dehydrated so try to drink before you are thirsty. Water is the most reliable fluid for re-hydration but can be boring so add a squeeze of lime to make it more palatable. Squash and other sugary drinks, if too concentrated, require your body to add water to them so that they can be absorbed. This obviously increases your dehydration problem. If you feel bloated you are probably drinking too much and may be prematurely flushing electrolytes from your body. Urine will run clear or straw coloured when your body is well hydrated and become progressively 'yellowed' as you dehydrate. A useful way to keep water-carrying bladders cool is to put a wine cooling 'jacket' from the freezer around them.

SPORTS/ENERGY DRINKS

The logic of sports drinks is easy to understand. They give the body a drink of water with fuel dissolved in it. You can go on far longer without putting in fuel than you can without putting in water. Never refuel at the expense of re-hydrating. Sports drinks that replace energy to refuel you necessarily have high concentrations of simple and complex sugars dissolved in them. Such drinks can dehydrate you further.

High concentration energy drinks are therefore not suitable for long, hot rides because they can increase your thirst, not quench it.

High-energy drinks are useful for replacing energy you have used at the end of a ride. It is a common misconception that they will give you energy before exercising. They can have a reverse effect by using up valuable water in the body and drawing blood away from muscles into the stomach thus impairing performance.

BODY REPAIR

NUTRITION

A common experience of riders who go on high activity holidays is that they appear to have boundless energy for the first few days but suffer a drained, under-powered feeling for a few days after that. This is usually because people go away with well-rested muscles saturated with stored fuel allowing you to ride particularly well for the first few rides. Once depleted, the sudden drop in available fuel plus the added build up of toxins and tightening associated with muscle fatigue means that, by the second or third day, you not only have less fuel to burn you are also less agile. This is especially true if you aren't used to being on your bike for long periods. Even if you keep fit by running or going to the gym, your 'riding' muscles may be unaccustomed to the high demand you are placing on them.

In order to get the most out of your riding, good nutrition is of major importance. As a general rule of thumb fresh fruit and vegetables are incredibly important and sometimes sacrificed by mountain bikers who try to maximise their carbohydrate and protein intake (steak and chips, spaghetti, fried breakfast) in order to refuel. During exercise your muscles are microscopically damaged and filled with toxins. The best materials to help them recover are found in salads, vegetables and fruit. Fresh produce also contains the electrolytes and minerals your body uses up. These food stuffs also have high water content that assists the re-hydration process whereas carbohydrates, proteins and fats all use up water in the digestive process.

Healthy balanced meals soon after exercise will ensure you repair and recover quickly and are able to enjoy the next ride. When you are exhausted, it's far too easy to sit down and rest neglecting the proper replenishment of your body's resources. There is a 'window of opportunity' after exercise of about 30 - 60 minutes when your body is most receptive to restoring nutrients and energy.

BODY REPAIR

STRETCHING AND FLEXIBILITY

WHY STRETCH? Watch an agile creature such as a cat for any length of time and you will notice that before they do anything strenuous, they stretch. But stretching isn't just for pussies! To get the most out of your body you need to keep it serviced.

A properly stretched muscle can contract more efficiently so it uses less energy and can contract harder, faster and for longer. Disciplined stretching can also help improve your bodily co-ordination and improve the shape and tone of muscles keeping healthy fibres in place and ensuring damaged fibres re-grow in the correct direction. It is important not to 'bounce' during stretching as this does not have the same effect as a held stretch. Holding a stretch conditions the muscle to being in an elongated position so that it can return to this position more easily during exercise.

WARMING UP

Stretching is not warming up. Warming up means raising your core temperature, increasing your heart rate and circulation. This increases blood flow to the muscles raising their temperature making them ready for stretching. A 'cold' stretch i.e. before you have warmed up, can cause damage. In fact, the best time to stretch is after exercise. A general warm-up should begin with joint-rotations. By rotating all joints you 'oil' the joint surfaces with a coating of synovial fluid. This lubrication increases the ease of movement and decreases wear. Perform slow circular movements, clockwise and anti-clockwise. Remember your fingers and knuckles, wrists, elbows, shoulders, neck, waist and hips, legs, knees, ankles, toes. After you have performed the joint rotations, try to perform at least five minutes of low intensity aerobic activity to 'get your blood pumping'.

WARMING DOWN

At the end of exercising or a long ride, a warm-down is extremely important. A warm-down is essentially a warm-up in reverse. You should try to perform at least five minutes of slow cycling at the end of a long ride just to let your heart rate settle. Stretching after exercise is a superb way of minimising muscle fatigue and soreness. Stiffness is the result of lactic acid and other waste products built up during heavy muscle usage. Stretching can loosen the muscles and facilitate the removal of these toxins. If still in pain the next day a warm up can help. Massages are an excellent way to look after the health of your muscles. Massaging can help muscles by increasing blood flow, warming it up, improving circulation, relaxing it, relieving pain and cramp, removing metabolic wastes and help return fibres to their optimum shape and realignment.

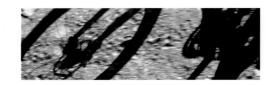

TRAVELLING WITH A BIKE

FLYING WITH A BIKE

Most airlines charge extra for bike carriage. When booking your ticket express your intention to travel with your bike and find out any hidden costs. Premiums vary wildly between airlines and there is seemingly no logic to these discrepancies. Interestingly golfers and skiers are not always charged for carriage of their sports kit so, if you are quoted a high price, it may be worth asking for a justification. If you pay for bike carriage before leaving the country or are told there will be no charge, it is advisable to get confirmation in writing as Spanish airports are notorious for charging you on the return journey in the absence of any written proof.

PACKING

Your bike is both valuable and often the very reason for your trip. Pack it well. Baggage handlers are not famed for their sensitivity so pack defensively. Remember you need to be able to repeat the packing process for the return journey so don't discard crucial bits like bubble wrap and packing material in your arrival excitement. Use a suitable container. Purpose built padded bags and flight cases are available from a variety of suppliers but are costly. If you can't afford one, it is worth asking your local bike shop for an empty box from a new bike.

REMEMBER TO TAKE:

☑ Helmet;

☑ Travel insurance;

☑ Spare inner tubes especially if bike shops are not accessible

☑ Trail tools, pump, patch kit, chain tool, multi-tool, allen keys etc;

☑ Spare chain, cables, brake pads and replacement drop out if your frame has a replaceable system;

☑ Spare tyres, take one thick pair to cope with gnarly areas;

☑ Body armour: lightweight shin and ellbow pads can be easily carried strapped to the outside of trail bags and can save you serious injury.

TRAVELLING WITH A BIKE

KEY TIPS:

FRAME
Remove wheels. Insert plastic braces into the forks and rear wheel space. These braces come fitted to new bikes and local bike shops can usually supply them. Otherwise clamp an old hub or piece of wood into wheel space. Remove handlebars from stem. Unscrew rear mech and leave loose but wrapped in a cloth/bubble wrap. Remove seat post & pedals. Wrap frame in an old blanket, sleeping bag or bubble wrap. Insert plastic blocks or cardboard between disc pads to prevent pistons closing if levers are accidentally pulled. Loosen retaining bolts on brake levers and gear shifters to allow them to rotate harmlessly if jolted. Leave chain on large chain ring to protect teeth.

WHEELS
Remove quick-release skewers and put plastic caps or tape card onto the axle ends and rear cogs. Either wrap wheels in a blanket or put card between wheel and frame. Remove a bit of pressure from the tyres to avoid problems at high altitudes.

TOOLS
Make a pile of all the tools you used to strip the bike and the bits you took off and remember to take all of these with you.

ESSENTIAL THOUGHTS:

Make sure you can carry your bike in its packing case and think about how far you have to travel at the other end. If you need a taxi, will you be able to fit it into one? If you are hiring a car, is it able to take your bike and all the passengers? Is there somewhere to store your bike once you arrive at your destination?

TRAVELLING WITH A BIKE

BIKE RACKS AND CARRYING BIKES ON VEHICLES

GENERAL SECURITY

Bikes attached to the outside of a vehicle can be easily tampered with and parts quickly removed. Think about where you park and store easily removable bits like tool kits, pumps, quick-release saddles and wheels inside your vehicle. Either lock frames to the rack or to each other (even if removed from the rack, two bikes or more locked together are harder to carry away).

UNSAFE LOAD

In practically every European country, being found carrying an unsafe load on your vehicle can lead to prosecution. A load can be deemed 'unsafe' for a host of different reasons. The most important things to think about are that the bikes aren't obscuring your vision, number plate or lights and that there is no danger of the bikes falling off, dragging or protruding from your vehicle in a dangerous manner.

INSIDE YOUR VEHICLE

Make sure they are well protected from rubbing against one another. Make sure that any load carried inside your car is safely secured. The forces involved in terms of forward momentum when you brake in an emergency situation are phenomenal. An unsecured bike becomes far heavier if it is thrown violently forward by emergency breaking.

ROOF - MOUNTED RACKS

In terms of versatility and all aspects of safety, racks on top of vehicles are in many ways preferable to other types. Bikes are harder for thieves to reach and they can usually be locked onto the rack. Bikes don't obscure your vision or lights. The roof is a sturdy platform and weight is more evenly distributed consequently heavier weights can be carried without unduly affecting vehicle performance. Often these types of rack carry the largest number of bikes. Bikes are more protected from scratching each other with wheel trays and clamps that hold bikes upright and separated. However there are drawbacks: bikes on roof racks are out of sight and easily put out of mind. They dramatically increase vehicle height and risk of damage from low carports, garages, bridges, trees, utility wires, etc. Think about putting a sign on your sun visor to remind yourself. They can affect vehicle performance due to increased drag especially in high winds and are generally more expensive than other types of racks.

TRAVELLING WITH A BIKE

REAR-OF-THE-VEHICLE RACKS

Whatever vehicle you have, there is likely to be a bike rack on the market that straps to the back of it. These types of racks offer a cheap and easy way to carry usually up to four bikes. However the use of these racks require the most thought. Think about the following:

☑ **Vision** - Remove wheels and seat-posts that obstruct vision. Make sure you can see vehicles coming from behind you and that they can see you. Ensure your reverse lights illuminate the ground behind you.

☑ **Lights and number plate** - Make sure your number plate and all lights are visible. Remember, it can be dangerous if other road users can't see you are braking or reversing not to mention the fact that having your lights obscured is illegal. It is possible to buy a light board and additional number plate to put over the last bike but these can be expensive so make sure you are properly advised when buying the rack.

☑ **Wider load** - Wheels and frames can protrude from the side of the vehicle making it wider. Adjust your mirrors to compensate. Your vehicle will be longer so you won't be able to fit into the same parking spaces. Make a mental note of the differences to your vehicle.

☑ **Increased weight** - Bikes on rear-racks increase your rear weight and can cause your suspension to sag. This sag is dramatically exaggerated as the vehicle bounces up and down at speed affecting the vehicle's performance. With this extra 'bounce' in mind, make sure there is sufficient clearance between bikes and ground and that your car is not overloaded so that it bottoms out on big bumps. Additionally make sure tyres and all other parts are clear from the exhaust pipes.

☑ **Fastening** - Always fasten then re-check strap tension after bikes are loaded for any loosening. Recheck them when you make stops during your journey and secure loose ends.

☑ **Bike protection** - strap-on racks are more likely to scratch bikes put too close together. Protect frames using foam blocks or pipe insulation/lagging. Make sure this is not liable to fly off in the turbulence of travel. Hook-ended bungee cords are handy for fastening bikes to racks. Make sure bikes aren't liable to flap against each other, bounce up and down, slide to the back of the vehicle and, obviously, fall off the back of the rack. Remember the forces the rack will be subjected to during travel can be far more severe than any shaking you can simulate. Some rear racks (especially for 4x4's) have mounting posts that fit to the rear tow-hitch mechanism. These structures can jut out from the rear of the vehicle like a lance and it is important to be aware of the potential hazard of driving a powerful vehicle and skewering structures, other vehicles and people with the rack.

THE MOUNTAIN BIKE IN SPAIN

Enjoying challenging singletrack requires good quality equipment. Make sure you have a bike that can cope with the rigorous demands of technical trails. If you do suffer a serious breakdown, use these translations to identify key parts of your bike in a Spanish mountain bike shop.

Before you visit an area, note whether there is a good bike shop nearby as indicated by the face symbol in the Bike Repair section. If the face is sad/red make sure you have plenty of spares. Alternatively check where your nearest TREK dealer is by looking on
www.trekbikes.com/home.jsp

Useful Phrases

Do you have	Tiene....................?
My.........is broken.	Mi..........es roto.
Do you do repairs?	Hace reparaciones?
Can you fix it?	Puede arreglarlo?
Whats that?	Que es eso?
How much is it?	Cuanto es?
I am lost.	Me he perdido.
Is there a bar near here?	Hay un bar por aqui?
Do you speak english?	Habla ingles?

English	Spanish
Puncture	Pinchazo
Pump	Inflar
Inner tube	Camara
Brake	Freno
Bent wheel	Rueda boleada
Energy bar	Barrita energética
Energy drink	Bebida energética

Saddle
Sillin

Seat post
Tija sillin

Brake cables
Cables del freno

Frame
Cuadro

Wheel
Rueda

Tyre
Neumático

Rear derailer
Cambio

Chain
Cadena

Front derailer
Desviador

THE MOUNTAIN BIKE IN SPAIN

Stem
Potencia

Handle bars
Manillar

Grips
Puños

Head set
Dirección

Gear shifters
Doblemando

Brake levers
**Manettas
de
freno**

Forks
Horquilla

Disc Brake
**Freno de
disco**

Pedals
Pedales

Hub
Buje

Crank set
**Caja
pedalier**

Wheel rim
Llanta

Quick-release skewer
Cierre rapido

TREK.

BIKE SPECIFIC ROUTES

THE CAMINO DE SANTIAGO

This route traverses the length of northern Spain from Roncesvalles in the Pyrenees to Santiago de Compostela in Galicia. The 750km route has been used since the dawn of Christianity by pilgrims making their way to Galicia to worship St. James. The pilgrimages reached their height in the middle ages but are still popular today with spiritual and non-spiritual visitors alike, including hikers, bikers and drivers. There are many publications detailing the various routes. The most popular is the 'Camino Frances' from Roncesvalles through the Navarran Pyrenees. Routes are clearly marked with blue signs with yellow scallop shells. In centuries past the scallop shell was evidence that you had made it to Santiago de Compostela; Galicia was the only part of Spain where scallops were harvested. Although singletrack can be found in the early stages, the trails can at times turn into busy highways.

BTT ROUTES

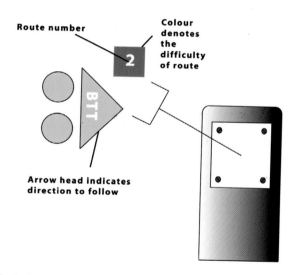

Route number

Colour denotes the difficulty of route

2

BTT

Arrow head indicates direction to follow

'BTT' stands for 'Bicicleta de Todo Terrano' (all terrain bike i.e. mountain bike). Spanish authorities in the North East are starting to build a network of marked out itineraries for off-road mountain biking. These routes are found in abundance particularly in Catalunya and the Pyrenees. The routes are sign-posted along their length with small, white plastic plaques embossed with two yellow circles and a yellow triangle; the trade mark of the rides. These signs indicate the direction of the route whilst a small number indicates the route you are following and the colour of the number indicates the difficulty of that itinerary. They are graded for difficulty like ski runs so that green is easy, blue - medium, red - hard and black very hard.

Each circuit has a host of indicator panels covering direction, hazards and locations of things such as bike washing points, showers, repairs and bike rental. Not all rides have these facilities but the benefit is that you can choose all details of your ride in advance.

Difficulty Indicator

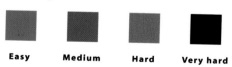

| Easy | Medium | Hard | Very hard |

In the areas where they operate, the tourist offices have plenty of leaflets available with detailed instructions of the routes and all they have to offer. On the whole these routes are well researched and equally well sign-posted. They also try to take you past points of local interest and facilities that you will need including service points and places to rest and eat.

BIKE SPECIFIC ROUTES

VÍA VERDES- GREENWAYS.

The Vía Verdes are a network of routes across the whole of Spain using disused and abandoned railway lines. These have been converted into pathways for non-motorised traffic and cater for pedestrians, cyclists, horse riders and people with reduced mobility. The programme was started in 1993 and has gone from strength to strength under the leadership of the Spanish Railways Foundation. This protection and preservation of the environment has promoted ecotourism in lesser known parts of the country and is a model for other European countries to emulate. Unemployed local people are being paid to create signposts and derelict stations are being turned into restaurants and bike hire shops. To date over 1000 km of routes have been renovated for public use and, though the routes do not connect across the whole of Spain, they do allow you to penetrate certain remote areas. As they follow the routes of old railway lines the gradients are not going to excite, rather they allow miles to be covered passing over bridges and viaducts, through tunnels and stunning scenery. If you want to make a holiday out of the Vía Verdes you can go on the 'Magic Tour' which takes place twice a year and whisks you around Spain by train, bus and bike. Vías Verdes (00 34 911 511065; Email viasverdes@ffe.es).

VÍA DE LA PLATA- THE SILVER ROUTE.

When the Romans first explored Spain their aim was to develop trade routes, specifically gold and silver from Spanish mines to Rome. One of the most productive deposits of silver was in Asturias and the booty had to be sent south through Castilla Y León and Extremadura to Seville. From here it was sent by boat to the Mediterranean. A road was built, lined with stone boulders and covered with stone slabs and the

Vía de Plata or Silver Route was born. The passage links places of archaeological interest (Itálica just outside of Seville and the

amphitheatre, aqueducts and mosaics at Mérida) and although often eclipsed by the busy N630 highway, is the best way to experience the remnants of Roman Spain.

CAÑADAS/VÍAS PECUARIAS

You will see on numerous maps old drovers' paths, or 'Cañadas' marked with two lines of dashes to indicate their whereabouts. These outline cattle paths and sometimes Roman roads (Calzada Romana). As you would imagine with cattle paths, unless well used the trails can disappear. However, well-managed and marked trails do exist across Spain and can be fast paced and fun to take on.

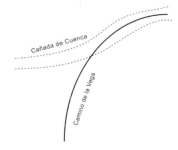

GR AND PR ROUTES

Large networks of sign-posted long distance paths criss-cross Spain. These GR routes or Gran Recorridos are characterised by avoiding roads and vehicle tracks and, more importantly, are usually made up of slim singletrack. They are not always maintained for their whole length but can provide some fantastic riding. The GR 7 for example is part of the E4 Mediterranean Arc, a path that runs from Greece via Bulgaria, Romania, Hungary, Austria, Germany, Switzerland and France the length of Spain, finally ending in Algeciras in Andalucía. Red and white stripes guide you along these pathways using the simple format shown in the diagram at the bottom of the page.

Another type of sign-posted route is the PR or Pequeño Receorrido. These are shorter paths often emanating from a village hub and can also make great riding as they are well-worn paths used regularly by walkers and often kept cleared and serviced by local authorities. The PRs use yellow and white markings to indicate the route.

GR and PR routes are marked along their length by markers that are painted onto anything including posts, fences, walls, rocks and trees. Although aimed at hikers they are often the best technical trails in a given area.

Continue

E - 4
GR - 7

Go left

**Wrong
Direction**

Go right

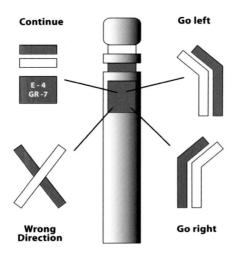

USING MAPS AND GPS

MAPS

When following our ride itineraries it is imperative that you have a local map with you to supplement the instructions in this guidebook. The rides explore potentially dangerous regions and we cannot condone people venturing into such exposed mountainous areas without a thorough understanding of the route they are following and any potential dangers. By requiring readers to plot their progress on a map we can be confident that in the event of an emergency they will be able to return safely.

Our ride instructions have been very carefully worded to contain just the right balance of information. There is sufficient detail to enable you to identify the route quickly and accurately on a map but they are not so detailed that the appearance of a new building or fork in the path will throw them into disarray. This in-built flexibility ensures that you get the maximum shelf life from your Trailrider Guide.

Given the importance of maps, we supply comprehensive details of which maps you need for each area, where to buy them and how easy they are to obtain. In areas where availability is poor, we recommend you purchase the maps you need before you travel. Order from www.stanfords.co.uk.

GPS

Accurate positioning of individual points on the earth's surface is made possible by reference to the geometrical system of latitude and longitude. Latitude parallels are drawn west-east and indicate the distance in degrees from Greenwich. Longitude meridians are drawn north-south and indicate the number of degrees either side of the prime meridian or equator. By referring to these co-ordinates and their subdivisions of minutes (1/60th of a degree) and seconds (1/60th of a minute) any place on earth can be located accurately.

We have included waypoints produced by a hand held Global Positioning System (GPS). These mark important landmarks and junctions on the riding itineraries. If you have a GPS system you can identify when you have arrived at the correct location. Without a GPS system you can still use the GPS readings to locate the point on most Spanish maps. Using the same methodology as grid reference usage with English Ordnance Survey maps, GPS co-ordinates can be used to locate points on most Spanish maps.

GPS points

N	W
1. **N40 19 881**	**W001 32 256**

The **N** refers to the vertical scale running up the right and left-hand edges of the map. Find the degrees and minutes eg **40°** and **19'** on the side of the map. You then need to divide the distance between 19' and 20' into 100ths and estimate where **881** is between these two numbers. Similarly the **W001°** and **32'** can be seen running along the top and bottom edges of the map and again you need to divide the bar between 32' and 33' into 100ths to find the **256**. Where these two points of reference meet is your bulls-eye!

SPAIN

Spain is a unique place. The culture and attitudes found here are subtly different to other European countries. Many civilisations have inhabited the Iberian Peninsular. Celts, Phoenicians, Romans, Visigoths, Jews and Moors have all left their mark. Some co-existed for long, peaceful periods allowing an intriguing melting pot of ideas, cultures and architecture to develop. It is easy to understand why man has favoured Spain as a place to settle.

The Moors who arrived in 711 A.D. had a great impact on Spain shaping its language, architecture and cuisine. The most highly cultured society of the European Middle Ages created a prosperous and tolerant empire known as Al-Andalus. Moorish/Arabic architecture remains in the form of castles, palaces, gardens and baths. Some of the best examples can be seen in the Alhambra Palace complex in Granada, the Mezquita temple in Córdoba and the Alcázar and the Giralda Tower in Seville. They also brought agricultural expertise with them and the vestiges of their time can still be seen in the terraces and irrigation systems of the Alpujarras. Another lasting imprint is flamenco music. Though traditionally seen as gypsy folklore many of the stories and tunes have apparent Arabic roots.

The Spanish Reconquista was complete when the Catholic Monarchs, Isabel and Ferdinand, finally quelled the Moorish infidels in 1492 A.D. With the help of the Inquisition they united the former taifas or mini kingdoms and Spain quickly developed as a powerful nation. In the sixteenth and seventeenth centuries it rose to its golden age when its South American colonies were providing vast wealth. The eighteenth and nineteenth centuries saw Spain's prominence decline with a succession of ineffectual kings. The painter Francisco Goya was the only hint of excellence of the time. The famous trio of modernist artists, Pablo Picasso,

Salvador Dalí and Joan Miró, flourished in anarchic Cataluña at the start of the 20th century. This period also saw the fantastic creativity of Antoni Gaudí, the innovative architect extraordinaire. More recently Spain suffered from long periods of extreme political unrest sparking conflicts including a bloody civil war (1936-39) which

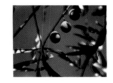

was won by right wing factions. Franco's notoriously tough dictatorship (1939 - 1975) governed the country until his death on 20th November 1975. Democracy was then quickly implemented allowing the country to modernise and many things that were illegal quickly became permissible. The country has developed rapidly ever since. It is now comprised of autonomous regions which have their own distinctive cuisine, history, festivals, countryside and sometimes language. There is enormous cultural diversity between northern, southern, central and eastern Spain and these differences are reflected in the varied countryside - from the verdant Cornish-like rias of Galicia in the North to the only desert in Europe in Almería in the South. One common Spanish passion is the fiesta. Coastal and rural villages alike have their own particular annual fiesta or feria. Famous ones include the running of the bulls in Pamplona, the six day Feria de Abril in Seville, the Romería del Rocío weekender in Huelva, the explosive seven day las Fallas in Valencia and close by in Buñol, the Tomatina, a short but frantic tomato throwing event. Semana Santa (Holy week/ Easter) is a spectacular week long event with processions of life sized religous icons around towns. The

Andalucían towns and cities specialise. Another common but contraversial enjoyment is the corrida or bull fight. Most towns have a bull ring but the animals can also be chased through town (encierros).

Unfortunately Spain is overlooked as a land for food lovers largely because the Gastronomic Epicentre - France, overshadows it. The food and drink is characterised by using produce local to the region. For example wild boar stew from Castilla y León, Serrano ham from Andalucía, octopus and scallops from Galicia, baked cod from Valencia, sardines from Cádiz, gazpacho in Seville, cider from Asturias, sherry from Málaga and wine from La Rioja.

Spain's popularity as a seaside resort for international tourists has played an important part in its economic growth. The enviable climate of the coastal areas has made them a honey pot for millions who flock to the 'costas' every year. Buildings have been erected unchecked and the areas have become overpopulated and unsightly.

This has stimulated rural tourism as visitors seek to avoid these resorts in order to see 'The Real Spain'. This cultural change has meant mountain biking is an important part of rural and environmentally aware tourism. Inland Spain is relatively unexplored and a great place to enjoy a cycling holiday.

RIDING IN SPAIN

The Spanish are keen cyclists and there seems to be a groundswell of development within the mountain biking community. Old paths are being developed for cyclists, local authorities are investing in facilities and there are countless tour operators offering biking holidays throughout Spain's mountains. Spaniards are proud to show the international community what their countryside has to offer. If you can cobble together a few sentences in Spanish and chat to local riders, it is not unusual for them to invite you to join them on their weekend ride.

The sedate pace of life and the laid back disposition of the Spanish bestow many benefits on the visiting biker. In particular rights of way across private land are far more relaxed than elsewhere and it is rare to find anyone complaining that you are cycling across their property. Laughably it is usually ex-pats who fence in their properties. Spanish common law insists the public must be allowed access to waterways and coastal areas. This creates a wealth of riding possibilities as ancient paths access streams, lakes, rivers and coastlines.

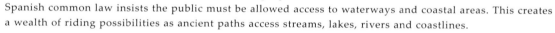

This massive country contains a relatively small population so there are great swathes of mountainous countryside to explore. What is more, the Spanish have a habit of living in close proximity to one another, which increases the amount of uninhabited land. Curiously this desire to live close to one another is not just a product of the Spanish being a sociable people; it is also a hangover from times when mainland Spain was a dangerous place to be alone. Roaming bandits, bears and wolves were a danger until relatively recently. Even today Spaniards are likely to come and camp right next to you in an otherwise empty campsite!

FACTS AND FIGURES

Spanish Tourist Information Offices in Great Britain: 22-23 Manchester Square, London W1M 5AP, 0207 486 8077.

Currency: Euro (1 Euro = 100 Centimos).

Capital: Madrid.

Population: 47,078,000.

Languages: Castilian Spanish (official) 74%, Catalan 17%, Galician 7%, Basque 2%.

Drive On: Right.

Alcohol Legal Limit: 0.8g per litre of blood.

Speed Limits: Motorway 120 kph, open road 100 kph and town 50 kph.

Religions: Roman Catholic 94%, other 6%.

Government Type: Parliamentary Monarchy

Internet Country Code: www. - .es

Telephone: 112 - emergency services. 1003 directory enquiries.

Major Airports: Málaga, Seville, Barcelona, Madrid, Almería & Alicante

Major Ports: Barcelona, Bilbao, Cádiz, Cartagena, Castellón de la Plana, Ceuta, Huelva, La Coruña, Málaga, Melilla, Pasajes, Gijón, Santander, Tarragona, València & Vigo.

Mountain Ranges: Cordillera Cantabrica, Montes de León, Pyrenees, Sistem Ibérico, Serania de Cuenca, Cordillera Central, Sierra de Guadarrama, Sierra de Montes de Toledo, Cordillera Betica & Sierra Nevada.

Elevation Extremes: Lowest point: Atlantic Ocean 0 m, highest point: Mulhacén, Sierra Nevada 3,482 m

Land Mass: Total Area: 504,782 km2, Land: 499,542 km2, Water: 5,240 km^2

Coastline: 4,965 km

RIDE RESORTS

FRANCE

La Coruña Oviedo Bilbao

Valladolid Zaragoza

PORTUGAL

Barcelona

MADRID

Cuenca

Valencia

Cordoba Murcia Alicante

Seville Granada

Malaga Almería

✈ City with
⬤ international airport
◯ Major town or city
⭐5 Destination location
and number
⭐ Bonus destinations

TRAILRIDER GUIDE

RIDE RESORTS

Each ride destination is listed according to the following format.

4 Colour and number of location to cross reference with map. Name of **Mountain Range** or **Natural Park** and the *Town/Village* that is the best base for riding.

---

1 **Montseny Natural Park**
Montseny

2 **The Pyrenees/Cerdanya**
Puigcerda

3 **The Pyrenees/Val D'Aran**
Vielha

4 **The Pyrenees/Val de Tena**
Formigal

5 **Picos de Europa**
Potes

6 **Sierra de Gredos**
Arenas de San Pedro

7 **La Pedriza Natural Park**
Manzanares el Real

8 **Sierra de Guadarrama**
San Lorenzo de El Escorial

9 **Serranía de Cuenca**
Cuenca

10 **Sierra de Albarracín**
Albarracín

11 **Sierra de Marina Alta**
Castell de Castells

12 **Sierra de Espuña**
El Berro

13 **Cazorla Natural Park**
Cazorla

14 **Massif de Cabo de Gata**
San José

15 **The Alpujarras**
Bubión

16 **Sierra Nevada**
Güéjar-Sierra

17 **Ardarles Natural Park**
El Chorro

18 **Sierra de Grazalema**
Grazalema

19 **Balcón de le Serranía**
Gaucín

Bonus Destinations
Barbate and Alcalá de los Gazules.

Northern Spain

MONTSENY
NATURAL PARK

SIERRA DE MONTSENY
BARCELONA - CATALUÑA

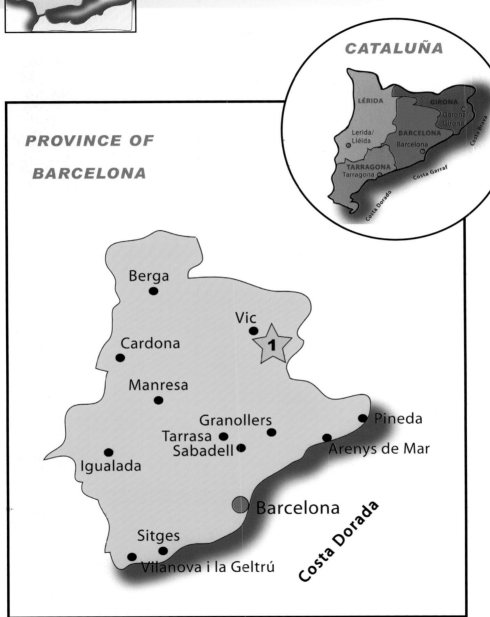

PROVINCE OF

BARCELONA

CATALUÑA

LÉRIDA
GIRONA
Gerona/
Girona
Lerida/
Lléida
BARCELONA
Barcelona
Costa Brava
TARRAGONA
Tarragona
Costa Garraf
Costa Dorado

Berga

Vic

1

Cardona

Manresa

Granollers
Tarrasa
Sabadell
Pineda

Igualada
Arenys de Mar

Barcelona

Sitges
Costa Dorada
Vilanova i la Geltrú

MONTSENY NATURAL PARK

NORTH EASTERN SPAIN

Location

The Montseny Natural Park covers 30,120 ha. and is found just to the north west of Barcelona in Cataluña. Although only a few kilometres from Barcelona, the park is kept isolated by the painfully slow access roads. It does get busy during weekends and holiday periods but the hillsides easily absorb this influx. You can wander into the most unlikely looking hostal and find a warm, friendly welcome, backed up by good food, wine and beds. Santa Fe offers slightly more than Montseny but a wider range of restaurants can be found in the larger towns that cater for tourists such as Arbúcies, Viladrau and Aigua Freda.

General Background

The park is characterised by the steep contours of its mountains. These vertiginous slopes are particularly appealing because of the mixture of different rock types and trees. Gullies are tucked into the deeply furrowed hillsides and kept secret by dense, mixed woodland. It is easy to see why the area is known for its witches. Oaks and pines inhabit low-lying areas and, above 1000m, beech groves and firs are found. Autumn is a colour festival as the chestnut, beech and oak trees change. Good food is important to the locals and their dishes are typically Catalán. Some specialities to try are jugged boar, wild mushrooms and stewed veal.

The Weather

Weather here is changeable. Spring and summer can be hot but there is a particularly extreme temperature swing from the peak summer heat to the cool temperatures of autumn. Autumnal weather begins to arrive at the end of August. Winter is particularly harsh when snow is plentiful. The woodland and many streams are strong reminders of the high levels of precipitation.

Protected Status

Riding is permitted in most areas of the park provided you don't deviate from existing footpaths. However, the authorities do not permit you to ride on the GR route or other footpaths that go over the Turo de l'Home. This is because it is too dangerous and they don't want to have to come and get you!

Local Dangers

Gradients are steep and littered with rocky debris. The slate and granite surfaces offer good traction in the wet but are loose when dry. Conversely the limestone rocks are slippery when wet but good when dry. Therefore be mindful of the surface you are on. This is especially important because you can so easily generate speed on the steep slopes. Tight zigzag turns are common place and this makes losing traction on the bends easy but unwise as a fall could send you over the edge of some perilous drops; not for the faint hearted. Good brakes and good sense essential.

Mountain Range
Serralada Prelitoral Catalana Coastal Mountains.

Highest Peak
Turo de l'Home, (1706m).

Getting There
Barcelona (70 km).
Renfe: Sant Celoni, Viladrau, La Garriga.

Nearest Town/City
Sant Celoni (15km)/Barcelona (65km).

Equipment Type
XC

Recommended Bases
Montseny, Camping Fontmartina.

Tourist Information
Natural Park Office at Fontmartina, www.diba.es/parcs, p.montseny@diba.es 938 475 102.

Ride Guides
None, but there is a bike club - Club Ciclista Corró D'Amunt, 938 710 423.

Body Repair
Surgery, Santa Celoni.
Red cross, 972 877 060.

TIGHT ZIG-ZAGGING TURNS,
PERILOUS DROPS AND LOOSE
SURFACES - GOOD BRAKES AND
GOOD SENSE ARE ESSENTIAL

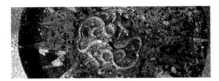

PROS + CONS
+ Close to Barcelona
+ Good in high summer
+ Challenging rides
- Early autumn
- Harsh winter
- Difficult access

☑ Equipment

Light, full-suspension, cross-country equipment is what you need.
Tough tyres are required to cope with the rocky surfaces. Good brakes
are most important for the intense descents. Wear tough clothing to
protect from the elements as well as the possibility of a fall.

XC Cross-Country

There are a number of organised bike routes set up by 'La Selva BTT
Centre' that start in the town of Sant Hilari Sacalm just to the north
of the park. Find out more at www.ccselva.org/turisme.

FR DH Freeride and Downhill

If you can get a lift up to the Coll Formic and someone to pick you
up at the bottom, there are good descents off this high peak. The GR
routes and footpaths in the woods around the Fontmartina campsite
provide some interesting trails for the freeride fraternity.

◉ Local Observations

Decide where you want to be based in advance because accessing other
parts of the park is frustrating. Somewhere that is only 5 kilometres
away as the crow flies can be many times that distance by road as you
meander backwards and forwards. You will need insect repellent, as
there are over 10,000 species of invertebrates natural to the area.

Hiking is very popular in the area and this means there is a well-developed backbone of singletrack. However, many of
these are impassable to bikes. There are two GR routes in the park. These are worth exploring. The GR2 runs through
Eva, El Brull and Aigua Greda and the GR5 starts at Campins going via Fontmartina, Montseny and the Calma Plain to
Aiguafreda. This is really a cross-country location where the uphills can go on for hours testing your tenacity. The
steep, snaking downhills are well suited to lightweight bikes and riders who know how to execute racing corners.

Maps ☺
Series: Montseny Parc Natural, Diputació Barcelona,
1:25,000. Buy in the Natural Park Office at
Fontmartina (10am-4pm week days).

Banks ☺
Montseny.

Fuel ☹

Bike Repair ☹

Bike Hire ☹

Other Activities
Hiking, horse riding, picnicking!!

Day Off
You have to go to Barcelona. Gaudi created the
must see 'La Sagrada de Familia' church and the
beguiling Parc Güell. Wander along the famous 'La
Rambla" street. Take the funicular to the top of
Mount Tibidabo and view the city.

Best Riding Times

J F M A M J J A S O N D

MONTSENY RIDES

Ride 1: El Convent Paig Gros

↔ 36km

⧗ 1 day

🍴 ■

💧 ■

⊡ ☺

GPS points

N	W
1. *N41 47 225*	*W002 27 331*

There is a superb playground of trails to be found just beyond Santa Fe. The toll road that runs between the Convent just outside of Santa Fe all the way down to Arbúcies is an excellent spine road to use for exploring this wooded valley. Start at the Centre D'Infoacio Can Casades information centre at Santa Fe. Head north-west towards Sant Marçel along the main road for 1.7km then turn right onto the toll road at (GPS 1). After 100m you pass the Convent Paig Gros. Follow this clearly defined sandy track to Arbúices.

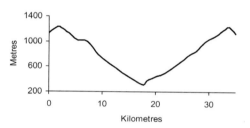

Ride 2: The E1 around the Escola De Natura de Can Lleonart

↔ 7km

⧗ ¼ day

🍴 ■

💧 ■

⊡ ☺

GPS points

N	W
1. *N41 46 488*	*W002 27 908*

Take the main road into Santa Fe. At the Centre D'Infoacio Can Casades find the Escola De Natura de Can Lleonart, which is located behind the information centre (GPS 1). From here a well-marked route called the E1 begins. Green metal posts that have red and white bands painted at their tops mark out the route. Follow these markers. Although the route is extremely technical in places there are some excellent sections.

YOU WILL NEED INSECT REPELLENT
AS THERE ARE OVER 10,000
SPECIES OF INVERTEBRATES
NATURAL TO THE AREA

Ride 3: Fontmartina to Tallabou

↔ **13km**

⧗ **½ day**

Ⓣ ■

◉ ■

▣ ☹

GPS points

N	W
1. **N41 45 383**	**W002 25 685**
2. **N41 44 384**	**W002 26 985**
3. **N41 45 499**	**W002 26 957**
4. **N41 45 386**	**W002 26 317**

Start from the campsite Fontmartina. Head away from the campsite entrance and turn left onto the second of two footpaths after a few metres (GPS 1). Follow the track downhill through woods for 900m to a stream. Cross it and turn right at the fork just afterwards. 1.5km from the campsite the path ends at some stairs. Descend onto a road. Turn right on the road away from the Riera de Cìuret campsite and around a hairpin bend so that you pass the restaurant 'Can Riera de Cìuret'. Follow the road through the restaurant's car park. Follow the GR 5 markers along the main road for 2km then turn left onto a track (the 3rd left turning after the restaurant). Follow the GR 5 trail to Tallabou for 1.3km until you reach an open grassy area a few hundred metres before the town. A track comes uphill on your right to join the GR route you are on. Just before the two routes meet turn left (GPS 2) onto a track going steeply uphill. (If you miss the turn continue on to the village of Tallabou. Get onto the main road BV 5114 and follow it uphill to the road marker KM 14 BV 5114. Go into the large layby and pick up the vehicle track from here.) Go steeply up for 300m until a major vehicle track cuts across the route you are on. Turn left. After 300m is a junction. Continue straight on. 300m further turn right following signs for Estany d'en Viada. Ascend for 3km until you pass a pond on the left and soon after a small waterfall on the

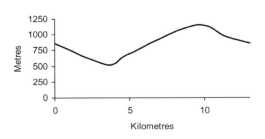

right. 600m from this stream turn left down a vehicle track with a chain across it (GPS 3). Ignore the immediate right and go straight on. 400m downhill, having gone around two big hairpin bends you come to a T-junction. Turn right going slightly uphill. Descend through five steep hairpin bends. After the fifth is a T-junction. Ignore the left to Rocanegra. Go through two more hairpin bends and on the third turn right onto an obvious singletrack (GPS 4). Follow this trail back to the campsite.

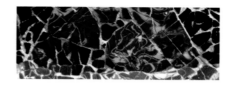

MONTSENY RIDES

Ride 4: La Cortada

◄► **28km**

⏳ **1 day**

🍴 ■

💧 ■

▣ ☺

GPS points

N	W
1. *N41 46 708*	*W002 22 820*
2. *N41 46 858*	*W002 20 760*
3. *N41 48 052*	*W002 20 850*

Start at Montseny. Head north out of town on the BV 5301 towards Brull. About 4.3km from town at the Km 18 road marker turn left into the layby (GPS 1) where a GR 5 route begins. Follow the red and white GR markers along this track for 4.7km to a junction (GPS 2) where the GR 5 route goes left downhill. Leave the GR route and turn right uphill. Soon after this you pass a house on the right and go under a power cable. After 2.1km pass a house called Les Mirones and 200m further another called La Cortada. 800m from here ignore the smaller track going right downhill and continue uphill. 3.5km from La Cortada you reach the main road going through the Coll Formic mountain pass where there is a restaurant. There are lots of GR routes here. Take the trail that goes up behind the restaurant - the GR 5.2 signed for La Pla de la Calma beginning at (GPS 3). 2.9km from the restaurant turn left at the junction. After 600m is a crude 4-way junction. Stay on the major route. A long descent follows. Turn left at the first major fork (ignoring the minor turning 300m before this). At the bottom of the descent you cross a bridge over the river in the valley bottom. Go right to return to the main road to take you back to Montseny.

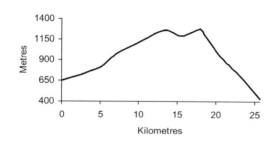

GULLIES ARE TUCKED INTO THE
DEEPLY FURROWED HILLSIDES
AND KEPT SECRET BY DENSE,
MIXED WOODLAND

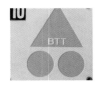

MONTSENY RIDES

Ride 5: Arbúcies to Sant Marçel

⬌ **35km**

⌛ **1 day**

🍴 ■

💧 ■

⛶ ☺

GPS points

N	W
1. *N41 48 387*	*W002 25 784*

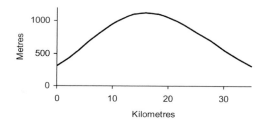

Parc de la Corbadora

Purpose built ride Number 10. There is a purpose built ride from Arbúcies to Sant Marçel and back. It is a black (i.e. difficult) route. From Arbúcies start on the GI 543 main road heading west out of town towards Espinelves. Before you leave town you reach a layby with a sign for the bar/restaurant La Corbadara and a sign saying 900m to the hospital. The first route marker is here. Look for a post with two yellow circles and a triangle that indicates the direction to take and a black number 10 underneath telling the route you are following. This route is hard because of the length and gradient of the climb. Follow the markers until you eventually reach the top of the climb where you briefly join the main road to St Marçel (GPS 1) before a long descent back to Arbúcies.

ACCOMMODATION

Being so close to affluent Barcelona, the park caters for every price range. A list of the extensive types of accommodation can be obtained from the Park information centre at Fontmartina.

Hostal La Cartoixa, Ctra de Palautordera a Seva, km 9.2, 938 475 011.
Hotel Sant Bernat ***, Finca El Cot, Ctra de Palautordera a Seva, km 20, 938 473 011.
Hostal Sant Marçal ***, Ctra de Sant Celoni a Viladrau, km 28.1, 938 473 043.
Hotel Can Barrina, Ctra de Santa Maria, De Palautordera a Seva, km 12.6, 938 473 065.
Hostal Santa Fe**, Santa Fe de Montseny, Ctra de Sant Celoni a Viladrau, 938 475 011.
Central camping, Fogars de Montclús, Fontmartina, 938 475 163.
Camping La Balma, Viladrau, 938 849 102.

OTHER AREAS TO EXPLORE

From Camping Fontmartina there is a host of small marked PR and GR tracks all around the campsite making this an ideal place to explore from. Visit the nearby mountain range of Montserrat. Downhill and trials events are held as part of the Copa Catalán 2002 near to Corró D'Amunt. The Federació Catalána de Ciclisme has up to date information on such events.

THE PYRENEES
PUIGCERDA

PUIGCERDA
CATALUÑA - GIRONA

PROVINCE
OF GIRONA

CATALUÑA

LÉRIDA

GIRONA
Gerona/
Girona

Lerida/
Lléida

BARCELONA
Barcelona

TARRAGONA
Tarragona

Costa Brava

Costa Garraf

Costa Dorado

2

Figueres

Cadaqués

Ribes

Ripoll

Olot

Gerona

Costa Brava

Palamós

Sant Feliu

Tossa de Mar

PUIGCERDÀ
NORTHERN SPAIN

Location

Puigcerdà is found in the Cerdanya depression, a large valley found between the Serra Cadí, Serra de Moixeró and the Pyrennees. It is the capital of the Cerdanya District and the first notable town you come to in the Eastern Spanish Pyrenees. Puigcerdà is close to Andorra, Barcelona and only 2 km from the French border making it a lively frontier town that receives a steady flow of human traffic.

General Background

This enormous valley is one of the largest in Europe and, at an altitude of 1200m, it is well exposed to the forces of nature. A host of minor valleys branch off from this massive valley. These little side valleys are home to a myriad of ski resorts. The transient population creates a strange 'border town' feel to Puigcerdà. There is a perceptibly different attitude here to other rural parts of Spain. A curt Northern European attitude prevails which is different to the usual laid back Spanish vibe. The area certainly has a pulse injected into it by party orientated 'radical dudes'. This youthful energy strongly influences the local shop owners who (again unusually for Spanish Mountains) have stocked up with all the latest gadgets, technologies and fashions. Although very European there is still a strong hint of the Catalan tradition.

The Weather

Rapid changes in weather are common and it is not unusual for cloudless skies in the morning to give way to storms by lunchtime. The altitude means the weather can turn unpleasant and you need to err on the side of caution when in the mountains. Snow begins to fall in earnest between November and December and lasts until March.

Protected Status

Outside of the beautiful Parc Natural Cadí Moixeró, there are no riding restrictions.

Local Dangers

Because the lowest level is 1200m and the rides venture much higher, the altitude is a problem and you need time to acclimatise. There can be extremes of weather at any time of the year including lightning, snow, hail, rain and heat. Respect for the elements is imperative.

Equipment

The lack of serious technical riding negates the need for bouncy bikes. Full suspension bikes are helpful if you are descending some of the rocky ski runs at La Molina. Tough terrain and viscous vegetation require a tyre of substance making thin or semi-slick treads inadvisable. Good weatherproof clothing must be with you at all times. As a minimum you should have a lightweight waterproof in your pack. There are good local bike shops to provide the right equipment.

Mountain Range
The Eastern Pyrenees.

Highest Peak
Tosa d'Alp (2537m).

Getting There
✈ Barcelona (180km), Madrid (614km).
🚉 Puigcerdà. Renfe (972 880 165).

Nearest Town/City
Puigcerdà/*Lleida (170 km)*.

Equipment Type

| DH | FR | XC |

Recommended Bases
Puigcerdà.

Tourist Information
Oficina Comarcal de Turisme de la Cerdanya (972 140 665) for information on accommodation, riding and events. www.cerdanya.org.

Ride Guides
La Fonda, 17538 Urús, 972 890 906, www.casafonda.com.

THE VAST VALLEY IS ONE OF
EUROPE'S LARGEST, RIDDLED
WITH A RIDICULOUS RANGE
OF ROUTES FOR RIDING

XC Cross-Country

This is a premier cross-country venue for those who like to spin
endlessly uphill to insane altitudes. One of the better routes is the
GR 107 route from Bellver de Cerdanya up to Refugi dels Conals.

FR DH Freeride and Downhill

There are some big mountains with ski lifts doing the hard work
for you. The most popular is the ski station at Super Molina. If
you are willing to do a bit of walking and lugging your bike over
rocks, there are some good descents from the top of La Molina.
Beware of maintenance work to the ski runs as it is often hard to
see excavations until your front wheel has been swallowed and
you are 20 metres down hill from your bike in a crumpled mess.

Local Observations

Nip across the border to the French supermarkets for your food
shopping. The low light pollution means it is a good area for
seeing stars and meteorite showers are especially visible in mid
August. It is hard to find cheap accommodation especially in
summer when the area is extremely popular with tourists.
Therefore it is best to base yourself outside of Puigcerdà.

This huge valley has an inordinate range of riding, from the flat
valley floor, which offers easy cruising to the substantial ski
slopes that provide well-marked out pistes. The tourist office can supply you with a fistful of leaflets for where
to find rides including mapped and signed, purpose built bike routes. Although there is a distinct lack of good
singletrack, there are few places as vast as Puigcerdà. Here you can cover staggering distances and heights as
well as enjoying a range of good facilities. The small ski resort of La Molina caters well for bikers in summer
(www.lamolina.com) and has a swimming pool at the cable car station to cool off after a ride.

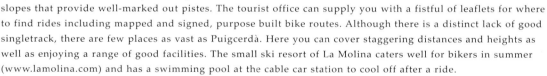

Maps 🙂
Series: Editorial Alpina, Cerdanya 1:50,000. Buy in
Puigcerdà.

Banks 😐
Puigcerdà.

Fuel 🙂
Puigcerdà.

Bike Repair 🙂
Esports Iris, Avda de França 16, Puigcerdà, 972 882 398.
Topbikes, Pla d'Arenes, s/n Ctra, N-152, Puigcerdà, 972
882 042.

Bike Hire 🙂
Esports Iris, Top Bikes, Ski Bike, Club Social I
Esportiu, La Molina.

Other Activities
Horse riding, hiking, quad bikes, archery, boating
(lakes near La Molina), pot-holing, 4x4 excursions,
hunting, gliding, white water rafting, cannyoning, rock
climbing. Skiing, cross country skiing and snow
boarding (La Molina/Masella).

Day Off
Visit Lleida. Go to the lively town of La Seu D'urgell. Take
the terrifying Port d'Envalira road pass into Andorra
(25km from Puigcerdà). Walk in the Serra del Cadí.

**Best Riding
Times**

J F M A M J J A S O N D

PUIGCERDÀ RIDES

Ride 1: Bellver de Cerdanya Circuit

↔ **30km**

⧗ **1 day**

GPS points

N	W
1. N42 18 570	W001 47 322
2. N42 18 563	W001 47 828

Start in the town of Bellver de Cerdanya. From the N 260 main road, cross the bridge over the El Segre River into Bellver de Cerdanya. After 500m turn right heading for the small hamlet called Talló (about 900m from Bellver de Cerdanya). This route becomes the GR 107. Follow it due south passing a church called Sant Serni (about 2.3km from Bellver de Cerdanya). Stay on the GR 107 and ascend for 9.4km to the Refugi dels Cortals (GPS 1). Continue past this building for a further 1.8km to a fork at 1761m (GPS 2) and turn left to Refugi del Serrat ignoring the right to Coll de Pendis. Soon the track starts to descend. Following the signs for 5.3km until you reach Refugi del Serrat. There is then a long descent until you come out in the town of Riu de Cerdenya. Head to the bottom of the town and follow the roads to the little town of Pedra and then onto Bor. Stay on the road and keep following the signs to Bellver de Cerdanya.

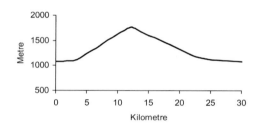

Ride 2: Coll de Turbains

↔ **31km**

⧗ **¾ day**

Start in Bagà. Head on the tarmac road to Gisclareny. Just after 2km you reach the St Joan Bridge. Carry on for 3km until there is a right turn onto a vehicle track that is signed to Sant Marti Del Puig. Stay on this track as it begins to climb more steeply and through pine woods. Eventually (after 13 km) you reach Col de la Bena. At the top, follow the track to the left as it starts to descend to Gisclareny. 7km from the Col de la Bena you go through the Coll de Turbians. Ignore the road to the left to the Escriga Pass (although this does return to Baga). 6km on from the Coll de Turbians pass the Font de la Vinya Vella. After a total of 29.5km you cross over the Vinya Vella and it is only 1km back to Bagà.

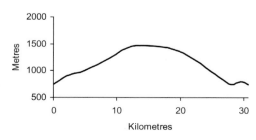

PUIGCERDÀ IS A WELL
SERVICED, ADRENALINE
ORIENTATED OASIS FOR
EXTREME SPORTS ENTHUSIASTS

Ride 3: Monestir de Bell-Lloc, Llívia

↔ **23km**

⧖ **1/3 day**

🍴 ▪

💧 ▪

🎯 😐

Start in Llívia (the Spanish town in France). This is a signed route with some markers to follow. Head north-west out of Llívia on the only major track heading to Villanova de les Escaldes. After 3.3km uphill to Villanova de les Escaldes follow the signs to the Monestir de Bell-Lloc (monastery). The monastery is the highest point of the ride (1685m). Follow the track around to the left in front of the monastery and descend for 2.35km to Brangolí. From Brangolí climb up to Feners passing near the interesting Celtic site called Dolmen de les Merruyes. Continue ascending past Feners until the track descends to Enveig. At Enveig take the main N20 road for 500m out of town then turn left following the signed bike route for circuit number 9. This track cuts out a big section of road riding and brings you to the village of Ur. Go through Ur back onto the N 20 for a short distance before turning left onto the D 618 road. Turn almost immediately right and pick up the cycle track back to Llívia.

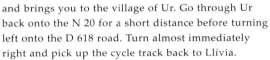

Ride 4: Above Queixans

↔ **14km**

⧖ **½ day**

🍴 ▪

💧 ▪

🎯 🙂

GPS points

N	W
1. *N42 22 532*	*W001 57 374*

In the centre of the town of Queixans there is a childrens' playground area and a church nearby. Take the vehicle track just before the church that climbs into the Serra De L'Orri hills that overlook Queixans. This is a popular ascent with walkers, bikers and vehicles. Ascend for 7km from town to a crossroads with a small pond on the right (it is possible to drive up to this point) (GPS 1). Local riders recommend exploring the various routes that can be found from this point.

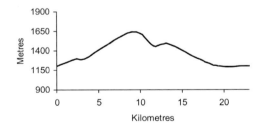

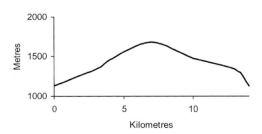

PUIGCERDÀ RIDES

LA MOLINA TELECABINA ALP 2500 SKI LIFT

6/11km

½ day

This is open daily in July and August from 10 a.m. - 16.45 p.m. (Tel 972 892 031). It takes you from 1740m up to 2340m.

From the top of La Molina Telecabina turn right out of the lift and follow the only vehicle track outside the building going downhill. Initially you descend with the cable car pylons on your right but you soon cross underneath these and zigzag beneath them down to the lake at the foot of the mountain. Pass the lake with it on your right follow the tarmac road to the lift station. An alternative route is to follow the above route to La Pleta where you turn off left. Stay on the vehicle track until you get to the Hotel L'Alp where you follow a road for 1.5km to a junction. Either go back to the start or take the smaller path that goes up to the lake before descending back to the start of the lift.

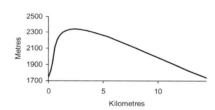

EVENTS: THE ALP GASTRONOMY FAIR IN MID SEPTEMBER. THE LIVE MUSIC FESTIVAL IN AUGUST AT LLÍVIA. BELLVER DE CERDANYA HAS AN ANNUAL HOT AIR BALLOON FIESTA AT EASTER. FIND OUT MORE AT WWW.PUIGCERDA.COM AND WWW.CERDANYA.ORG

OTHER AREAS TO EXPLORE

Soon to be opened-the La Cerdanya BTT/VTT cycling Centre: Sitesvtt@wanadoo.fr/.com which will have graded, clearly marked cycle routes all over the area.

The stunning Parc Natural Cadí Moixeró. You are stopped from riding anywhere but on the way-marked paths. These itineraries are all forest tracks and roads and you are not allowed to deviate from them. They are fairly tame but provide plenty of easy to follow routes.

As you leave Cerdanya heading west along the valley you eventually reach La Seu d'Urgell. This was part of the Olympic Games in 1992. Here there is a mountain bike course in the 'Olympic Parc Del Segre'. For information call 973 36 00 92.

The Val D'Aran and Val De Tena are two biking resorts geographically close to Puigcerdà that can offer everything that Puigcerdà is unable to deliver: decent, technical singletrack. They take a while to drive to because of the tortuous roads.

ACCOMMODATION

Contact Patronat Municipal de Turisme, Tel 972 880 542/www.puigcerda.com
Puigcerdà has an excellent but expensive campsite. A slightly cheaper and more charming campsite is found in Queixans - Camping Fontanals de Cerdanya.

Puigcerdà
Pension Prat, Puigcerdà, 972 880 261
Hostal Esatción, Plaça de L'Estació 2, Puigcerdà, 972 880 350
Hostal Alfonso, Carrer d'Espanya 5, Puigcerdà, 972 880 350
Hostal** Alfonso, Puigcerdà, 972 880 246
Hostal La Muntanya, Avinguda del Coronel Molera 1, 972 880 202
Hotel Avet Blau, Plaça de Santa Maria 14, 972 882 552
Hotel Sala, Carrer d'Alfons I 17, 972 880 104
Hotel Del Lago, Avinguda del Dr Piguillem, 972 881 000
Hotel** Del Prado, Puigcerdà, 972 880 400
Camping STEL, Ctra de Llívia, s/n, Puigcerdà, 972 882 361

Queixans
Camping Queixans, Cami Queixans a Urtx s/n, Fontanals de Cerdanya,
972 141 280, www.adv.es/queixanscamp;www.stel.es; Log cabins available.

Urús
Fonda Cobadana, Urús, 972 89 09 06

THE PYRENEES
VAL
D'ARAN

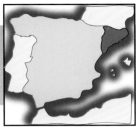

VAL D'ARAN
LLEIDA - CATALUÑA

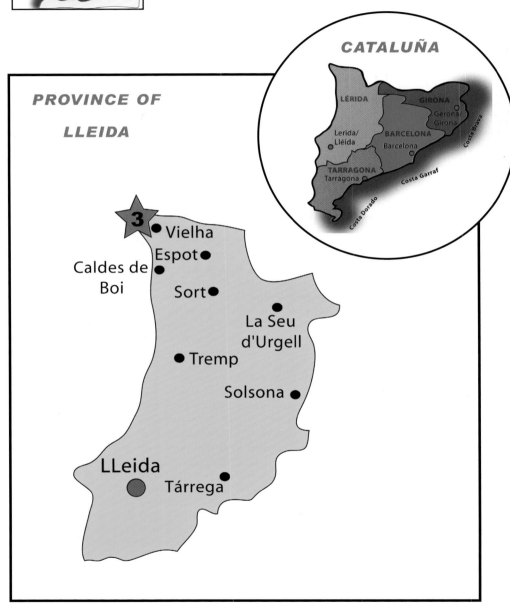

CATALUÑA

LÉRIDA
GIRONA
Gerona/
Girona
Lerida/
Lléida
BARCELONA
Barcelona
Costa Brava
TARRAGONA
Tarragona
Costa Garraf
Costa Dorado

PROVINCE OF

LLEIDA

3

Vielha

Espot

Caldes de Boi

Sort

La Seu d'Urgell

Tremp

Solsona

LLeida

Tárrega

VAL D'ARAN
NORTHERN SPAIN

Location

The Val d'Aran is in the Northern most part of Catalunya in the Pyrenees. It is a long, thin valley stretching for 35km with the Garona River flowing along its length. This relatively short valley ends in France but the river continues on until it empties into the sea at Bordeaux as the Garonne. The massive mountain summits that create this surprisingly corridor-like valley exceed 3000m and tower 2000m above the valley floor. This dramatic height difference creates some sensational scenery and wild weather.

General Background

Historically the valley was impenetrable, landlocked by the immense mountains. This isolation lasted for centuries and the farmers who populated the valley developed some unique cultural traditions that are neither French nor Catalan but Aranese. 50 years ago the Vielha tunnel (5.25km long) was built allowing the Baquèira-Beret ski resort to blossom and tourism to become the main form of income. Although skiing has transformed the valley with explosive force into one of the richest regions in Spain, the original charm remains unchanged. The old towns, although modernised, have kept much of their charisma. The area is famous for its glacial scenery in the

Parc Nacional d'Aiguestortes I Estany de Sant Maurini. It is without doubt the awesome surroundings that you will remember most about the Val d'Aran. Despite the presence of a major ski resort and massive hydroelectricity plants, the scale of the valley utterly dwarfs the presence of mankind.

The Weather

Val d'Aran is the only Atlantic-facing valley in Catalunya. This orientation assures a good thickness of snow in winter as wet Atlantic weather is quickly funnelled up the valley. Snow falls as early as October and can last all year on higher peaks. It gets cold early in the year making the riding season short. Autumn arrives in August when most other areas are in the height of summer. Changeable conditions are experienced throughout the year and there is often plenty of rainfall. The Val d'Aran is a good peak summer destination when rainfall is fairly low and temperatures are pleasant.

Protected Status

Riding is permitted wherever it is safe. In the National Park normal rules apply - you cannot ride on footpaths.

Local Dangers

When you ride, go prepared for bad weather even on the bluest skied days. The combination of high altitude and harsh weather makes using good mountain sense imperative. Some of the singletrack is extremely technical and difficult to follow so only attempt the harder rides if you are confident of your ability.

Mountain Range
The Catalan Pyrenees.

Highest Peak
Pic de Comaloforno 3033m.

Getting There
Toulouse (166km), Barcelona (350km).
Montrejeau (60km), Lleida (160km).

Nearest Town/City
Vielha/ Lleida (160km), Toulouse (166km).

Equipment Type
XC

Recommended Bases
Vielha or Salardú.

Tourist Information
Torisme Val d'Aran, Ctra Gausac, 1, Vielha, www.torismo.aran.org. Oficina de Torisme de Bossòst, Eduard Aunos, s/n Bossòst, 973 647 279. Oficina de Torisme de la Val d'Aran, Vielha, 973 64 01 10.

Ride Guides
See section on BTT Centres on page 24.

Body Repair
Hospital in Vielha, 973 640 004/6.

EXPECT TO BE FRUSTRATED,
DISPIRITED THEN UPLIFTED
AND AMAZED BY THE
INSPIRING IF SCARY RIDING

☑ Equipment

Any bike you take will be hammered by these hills though you may care more about your body lasting than your bike. Cross-country bikes are a sensible choice because of the climbs and distances involved, but freeride pedals are advisable because of the wet, slippery, rock strewn paths.

XC Cross-Country

Cross-country trails are abundant. If you are prepared to do a fair bit of road riding as well you can link together some long rides through excellent scenery. The BTT rides tend to favour wide tracks and open up the valley.

FR Freeride

The PR 111 that descends from near the Tuc de Salana peak (2483m) down to the village of Gessa is superb (if a little tricky to follow). The thin trail sits on a narrow ledge that starts at about 2000m and, in places, there are drops of 700m straight down into the Val de Valarties below. Inspiring but scary riding.

DH Downhill

Ski lifts stay open during the summer at the Baquèira Beret ski resort so, if you want effortless uphills, explore the chair lifts at Bosc, Mirador and Bonaigua.

◉ Local Observations

It is important to note that currently there is no decent bike shop in the area. Multi-purpose sports shops are the best you will find that stock basic biking equipment. A plentiful supply of spares is therefore advisable.

Local authorities have done a great deal to welcome mountain bikers to the area. Consequently it is one of the best areas in Spain for purpose built bike trails. The 'Centres BTT/FCC' organisation have created their own clearly marked and graded routes. There is a booklet accompanying the Alpina Maps for the area that include a host of riding itineraries and mountain biking literature is obtainable in abundance from the numerous tourist offices, hotels and campsites.

Maps ☺
Series: Editorial Alpina, Val d'Aran, 1:40,000. Buy in Vielha.

Banks ☺
Vielha.

Fuel ☺
Vielha.

Bike Repair ☹
Bodysport, Aptos Sapporo II, Vielha, 973 640 444.

Bike Hire ☺
See secton on BTT Centres (Pg 24).

Other Activities
White water rafting, canoeing, kayaking, canyoning, rock climbing, archery, hiking, horse riding, quad bikes, ice-skating, golf, fishing, para-gliding, Skiing (Baquièra Beret has 53 pistes).

Day Off
White water rafting on the Noguera Pallaresa river. Take in the impressive landscapes of Catalunya's National Park- D'Aigüestortes i Estany de Sant Maurici. Enjoy the countless après ski facilities.

Best Riding Times

J F M A M J J A S O N D

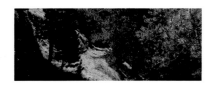

VAL D'ARAN RIDES

Ride 1: Around the Tuc de Salana peak

↔ **29km**

⧖ **1 day**

Y ■

▲ ■

⧉ ☺

GPS points

N	W
1. N42 42 405	W000 54 185
2. N42 39 614	W000 54 069

Head through Salardú on the main road (C 28) heading up the valley, away from Vielha. At a bend in the road in the middle of Salardú turn right by a Caixa Bank and Totos bar (GPS 1) following signs for Bahns de Tredos. After 3km pass the Barratage D'Aiguamog reservoir. Continue for 5km to a car park and hotel at Bahns de Tredos. Here the tarmac road ends. Follow a vehicle track past the front of the car park entrance ignoring the left turn just beyond it. Climb towards the Refugi Colomers. After about 4km from the car park you pass a small footpath on your left leading to the Refugi Colomers. Although easy to miss, it is very popular with hikers and vehicles deliver walkers to this point. Once past this point the climb becomes steep and rocky. Keep ascending around the side of the Tuc de Salana peak until you finally stop climbing. Continue until the trail starts to descend. After a 2km descent turn right at the first major junction onto the PR 111 which is marked by yellow and white (GPS 2). Follow this route for about 1km until you cross a stream. Almost straight away turn left onto a slightly obscure singletrack always following the yellow and white markers. The trail clings to the side of a steep slope and you have to go through 2 short tunnels. The singletrack ends at a building. Continue up a flight of stairs then follow the trail away from the building. About 250 metres from the building the path becomes increasingly unrideable and eventually appears to end at an open grassy area where the markers are hard to follow. Search downhill to your left in the centre of this grassy area for yellow and white markers on stones and trees. Once located this trail downhill is very steep. It becomes increasingly obvious until you eventually join a vehicle track near the Refugi Forestal de Mont-Romies. Continue following the yellow markers and you descend on a vehicle track zig-zagging downhill back to the main road. Turn right on the main road to return to Salardú.

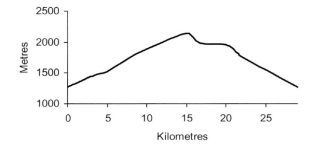

ANY BIKE YOU TAKE WILL BE
HAMMERED BY THESE HILLS THOUGH
YOU MAY BE MORE PREOCCUPIED
WITH PERSONAL PRESERVATION

Centres BTT/FCC - Val D'Aran

The Catalunya tourist board has built a robust and well-maintained network of marked routes for mountain bikes. They are known as 'Centres BTT'. 'BTT' stands for 'Bicicleta Todo Terreno' and there are about 100km of routes in the province. Information boards with maps and useful technical data are found at various reception, information and starting points.

There are 5 such reception points at:
Camping Caurca, Cami Paisas, Les 25540, Tel 973 647 045. deportur@arrakis.es;
Sports Area Bossòst, Dehòres 25550, 973 647 241;
Ice Hall, Av Garona 33, Vielha 25530, 973 642 864, palaidegeu@jazzfree.com;
Hostel Era Garona, Ctra Vielha, Salardú 25598, 973 645 271, www.aranweb.com/garona;
Baqueira 1500, Hotel Montarto, Camins, Salardú 25598, 973 639 091, www.aranweb.com/camins.

On the whole these routes are well researched and equally well sign-posted. The signposts consist of wooden stakes with small, white plastic plaques embossed with two yellow circles and a yellow triangle. This is the BTT trademark that you will quickly become familiar with. The direction of the route is indicated by the point of the triangle whilst a small number indicates the route you are following and the colour of that number indicates the difficulty of that itinerary.

Green   =   Easy
Blue   =   Medium
Red   =   Hard
Black   =   **Very Hard**

The Val d'Aran has seven BTT routes: one green, two blue, three red and one black. Markers appear every 500 metres or so but they appear more frequently if there are junctions or changes in direction. Information and maps for all routes are readily available from the various dedicated centres and tourist offices. The BTT centres also provide bike rental, parking facilities and body and bike washing areas.

The BTT leaflets are titled 'discover the land' because the designers of the routes want you to enjoy both a good ride as well as seeing what the locality has to offer. Unlike the intentions of this guidebook, these routes are not specifically aimed at looking for excellent trails. Therefore you are purposely taken past all the important sites of historical interest. The quality of this area makes it difficult for the rides to be anything other than fantastic.

There are information points at the following locations:

Val d'Aran, Sarriulèra, 5, Vielha 25530, 973 640 110;
Tourist Office Bossòst, Eduard Aunòs, Bossòst 25550, 973 647 279;
Tourist office Les, Pl Dera Ajuntament, Les 25540, 973 647 303;
Tourist Office Salardú, Trauèssera Balmes, 2, Salardú 25598, 973 645 726;
Tourism Val d'Aran, Ctra Gausac, 1, Vielha 25530, www.aran.org.

VAL D'ARAN RIDES

Local GR and PR routes

As well as the Centres BTT routes, the Val D'Aran tourist board have also made a series of glossy mountain bike itineraries. There is a pack of 6 rides varying in duration and technicality. They pass through the stunning scenery on PR and GR routes and give you a little blurb about the area you will ride through. They are an excellent (and free) resource. Look out for them in all tourist offices and most camp sites.

METEOROLOGICAL INFORMATION IN THE AREA IS FOUND AT WWW.GENCAT.ES/SERVMET OR AT WWW.INM.ES . ROAD INFORMATION CAN BE OBTAINED FROM WWW.DGT.ES.

OTHER AREAS TO EXPLORE

The Val d'Aran is surrounded by some amazing Pyrenean riding. Practically anywhere you visit will have some good trails. The Valle de Tena in Aragón is relatively close and worthy of a visit for its exceptional singletrack.

ACCOMMODATION

The valley has the infrastructure to cater for all accommodation needs with an estimated 8000 beds. www.aran.org has a list of available accommodation. Take advantage of the many ski lodges keen to fill their rooms out of season. The most expensive area is Baquèira Beret where royalty come and stay. Cheaper areas are found lower down the mountain such as Vielha, Salardú and Arties.

Vielha
Hotel El Ciervo, Pl Sant Orenc, 3, 25530 Vielha, 973 640 165, elciervo@arraquis.es.
Hotel Aran, Castiero, 5, 25530, Vielha, 973 640 050, hotelaran@jazzfree.com.
Hotel Ribaeta, Pl Coto Marzo, s/n, 25530, Vielha, 973 642 036, hribaeta@terra.es.
Aparthotel Serrano, Sant Nicolau 2, 25530 Vielha, 973 640 150, hssl@sispromat.com.
Aparthotel, Refugi D'Aran, Av, Garona, 27, 25530, Vielha, 973 643 002, refugiaran@wanadoo.es.

Arties
Parador D'Arties, Ctra Baquèira, 25599 Arties, 973 640 801, arties@parador.es.
Hotel Besiberri, Deth Fort, 4, 25599 Arties, 973 640 829.
Hotel Val Arties, Major 3, 25599 Arties, 973 644 364, valarties@aranweb.com.
Camping Era Yerla D'Arties, 2a Ctra Baquèira, Km 38, 25599, Arties, 973 641 602.

Baquèira
Hotel Val de Ruda, Ctra Beret, 25598, Baquèira, 973645 811.
Hotel Montarto, Baquèira 1500, 25598, Baquèira, 973 639 001.

Bossòst
Hotel Batalla, Urb Solei dera Val, s/n, 25550 Bossòst, 973 648 199.
Hotel Vilabossost Pietat, 33, 25550 Bossòst, 973 648 246.

Salardú
Hotel Colomers, Dera Mola, 8, 25598, Salardú, 973 644 556.
Hotel Garona, Ctra Baquèira, 25598, Salardú, 973 645 010.
Auberja Garona, Ctra Baquèira, 25598, Salardú, 973 645 271, eragarona@aran.org.

Les
Auberja Matacabos, Sant Jaime, s/n 25540 Les, 973 648 048, matacabos@aran.org.

Pònt D'Arros
Camping Verneda SL
Crta N 230 km 171, 25539 Pònt D'Arros, 973 641 024, www.campingverneda.com.

THE PYRENEES
VALLE DE TENA

VALLE DE TENA
HUESCA - ARAGÓN

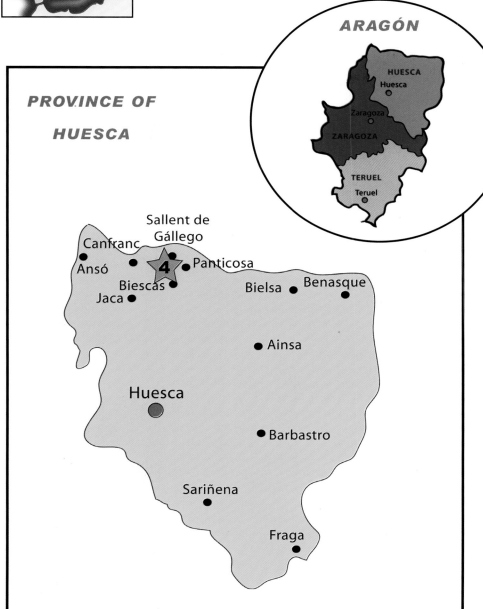

ARAGÓN

PROVINCE OF

HUESCA

HUESCA

Huesca

Zaragoza

ZARAGOZA

TERUEL

Teruel

Sallent de Gállego

Canfranc

Ansó

Panticosa

4

Biescas

Jaca

Bielsa

Benasque

Ainsa

Huesca

Barbastro

Sariñena

Fraga

VALLE DE TENA
NORTHERN SPAIN

Location

Valle de Tena is a stunning region in the Western Pyrenees dotted with glaciated lakes (ibóns) and a cluster of little known ski resorts that nestle in the Gállego river valley. It is on the doorstep of France and the village of Formigal is just 5km from the border. Although beautiful, the area manages to evade hoards of tourists. This is because the French resorts and the nearby Parque Nacional De Ordesa y Monte Perdido (arguably home to the most spectacular scenery in the whole of the Spanish Pyrenees) attract the lion's share of the tourist industry. Therefore, although staggeringly beautiful, Valle de Tena is an overlooked venue and makes a perfect place for a summer biking break.

General Background

The area was a tranquil valley of poor farmers until the skiing industry started to bring in money and development. Despite this modernisation, each village has developed slowly and they all remain attractive. The sheer scale of the mountains is breathtaking. Panticosa alone has 9 peaks above 3000m. The landscape is characteristically glaciated and there are momentous U-shaped valleys and glacial lakes whose blue waters are particularly startling. There are thermal springs at the Balneario de Panticosa whose granite-filtered water is used to cure various ills. Most importantly, the idyllic villages are home to some first class summer riding especially around Escarilla.

The Weather

Stormy Atlantic conditions tend to dump on these high mountains particularly on the steeper French side. When rain falls on the French side it causes a local, cold wind to spill down into Valle de Tena. In any event the region still receives a healthy amount of wet weather. Microclimates make weather prediction notoriously difficult. Storm fronts hit unexpectedly or not at all as the localised winds and altitudes play havoc with air-streams. Snow falls as early as October and on the higher peaks it can last all year. It gets cold early making the riding season much shorter than elsewhere in Spain.

Protected Status

Riding is permitted anywhere.

Local Dangers

It is surprising how the warm sun and lawn-like alpine meadows make you feel comfortable so that you never feel as exposed as you perhaps should. It is advisable to keep such flippancy firmly in check as conditions can change quickly and you can be a long way from anywhere when the weather turns. Be mindful of over-exposure to the strong sun. After a tough climb in the intense heat a swim in the reservoirs can be essential.

Mountain Range
The (Aragonese) Pyrenees

Highest Peak
Pico Clot de la Hount (3298m)

Getting There
Barcelona (350km), Madrid (450km), Toulouse (250km).)

Jaca (50km).

Nearest Town/City
Jaca (50km)/*Zaragoza (120km)*.

Equipment Type
XC

Recommended Bases
Formigal, Sallent de Gállega, Panticosa, Escarrilla.

Tourist Information
Valle De Tena Asociacion Turistica, Formigal, 974 490196, www.valledetena.com.

Ride Guides
Naturaleza y Aventura, Formigal, 974 490 046, www.naturalezayaventura.com

STAGGERINGLY BEAUTIFUL, TENA
IS HOME TO SOME SUPREME
SECTIONS OF SMOOTH-
SURFACED SINGLETRACK

PROS + CONS

+ Relatively undiscovered
+ Superb singletrack
+ Stunning natural beauty
+ Pleasant summer heat
- Short riding season
- BIG weather systems

☑ Equipment

There are no serious rocks and trail surfaces tend to be silt covered with relatively few technical sections to negotiate. Uphills are long. The need for big travel bikes with fat tyres is therefore minimal. Lightweight full suspension bikes or hard-tails are a sound choice and this is one of the few places where lightweight tyres are advisable. The riding tends to be on fast and smooth terrain. Being so high and isolated makes spare parts difficult to obtain. The English-run bike/ski/climbing shop in Formigal has surprisingly useful bits and pieces and good bike hire but don't expect to find ultra modern kit.

XC FR Cross Country and Freeride

There are many huge mountains covered by a networks of vehicle tracks. This makes Valle de Tena an ideal cross-country location. Although there are currently no operational lifts for mountain biking at the Formigal ski station, there are plenty of routes that are easy to identify. These provide tough cross-country rides. Free-riders should explore these vehicle tracks as well and keep an eye out for the paths that deviate from the main track for more adventurous downhills.

DH Downhill

There are plans to open lifts at the Formigal ski station to bikers. Currently the only operational lift is the bubble car at Panticosa that operates from the end of June to the beginning of September allowing pedal-free access to the World Cup Downhill course used in the 1990s. This is a great riding area but there is more potential as yet untapped.

◉ Local Observations

There are some very welcome lifts to take you and your bike up the mountains; there is the bubble car at Panticosa and a tourist train at Tramacastilla. There are also plenty of good vehicle tracks allowing you to access high regions relatively easily. On the local 1:40,000-scale map there are marked bike routes. The black BTT 'por pista' marked routes are vehicle track routes. The red BTT 'fuera de pista' routes are literally translated 'off the beaten track' so should be hard going singletrack. The low frequency of trees at these altitudes means that you can spot good trails from a long way off. It is worth carrying some binoculars so you can check things out from afar.

📍 Maps ☺
Series: Editorial Pirineo, 1:40,000 No.3, 'Valle De Tena - Vignemale'. Buy in most village shops

$ Banks ☺
Most towns.

🛢 Fuel ☹
One just outside Formigal and one just below Escarrilla.

🔧 Bike Repair 😐
Ski Total S A, Sallent de Gállego, 974 490 184.
The sports shop in Panticosa has inner tubes.

🚲 Bike Hire ☺
Ski Total S A and Naturaleza y Aventura (as listed).

👍 Other Activities
Hiking, climbing (indoor and outdoor), helicopter trips, horse riding, swimming, ice skating, rafting, windsurfing, canoeing, boating, ab-sailing, zip-lining, paragliding, skiing, fishing.

Day Off
Visit the Parque Nacional De Ordesa y Monte Perdido. Bathe in the healing properties of the granite-filtered, thermal springs at Balneario de Panticosa.

Best Riding Times

J F M A M J J A S O N D

VALLE DE TENA RIDES

Ride 1: Ibón de Tramacastilla

↔ **24km**

⧗ **1 day**

🍴 ■

🔥 ■

⬚ 😐

GPS points

	N	W
1.	N42 42 952	W000 19 836
2.	N42 43 276	W000 22 253

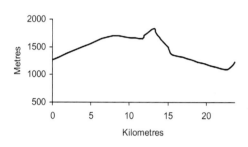

From Tramacastilla de Tena take the vehicle track to the reservoir called 'Ibón de Tramacastilla'. This track is the first left turn on the road between the towns of Tramacastilla and Sandinies. Follow the route used by the tourist 'train'. A barrier at GPS 1 blocks the track. Continue ascending from here for 5km until you reach the first reservoir - Ibón de Tramacastilla. As soon as you reach this lake turn immediately right onto the singletrack around the edge of the water (GPS 2). Follow it until you reach a dam wall at the far end. Here a stream flows from this reservoir to the next and you need to follow the approximate direction of the stream around the corner to the second reservoir - Embalse de Escarra. There are a couple of hard to follow goat tracks between the two reservoirs. Once at the second lake, cycle along the right-hand bank following GR red and white markers to the far end of the valley. Just before the dam wall you pass a derelict building on your left. Cross over the dam wall to the far bank and turn right on the other side so that you head away from the lake. You need to walk up a short, steep rocky bank at the top of which there is a GR signed singletrack. After a few hundred meters is a sign posted junction. Turn left

uphill, signed to 'Collado de Pazino', ignoring the right signed to 'Escarrilla'. Climb the switchbacking singletrack to the summit then descend on singletrack to a gate. Follow the vehicle track on the other side of this back to the main road. Turn right on the main road. Follow it downhill through the tunnel just before Escarrilla and back to the start.

LAZE THROUGH THE ALPINE
MEADOWS FEELING MASTERFUL
BUT BE MINDFUL OF OVER-
EXPOSURE TO THE SUN

PANTICOSA SKI STATION

Ride 2: 1996 World Cup Downhill Course

↔ **8km**

⧗ **¼ day**

Ψ ▢

🌢 ▢

▣ ☺

The telecabina operates during much of the summer. It is good value there being a day ticket available. There are also a number of different bike routes to follow.

This is a black BTT Por Pista marked bike route on the map. This was a downhill course during the 1990's on the world cup. Go up the telecabina and at the top go down the stairs, and as you look up the mountain with the top of the lift behind you the downhill piste is an obvious track to your left.

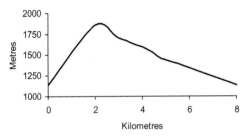

Ride 3 : Embalse de Búbal

↔ **16km**

⧗ **1/3 day**

Ψ ▢

🌢 ▢

▣ ☺

At the top of the Panticosa Telecabina turn right following the vehicle track on a long and steep zigzagging track down into the town of Hoz de Jaca. Follow the main road along the edge of the reservoir 'Embalse de Búbal' back to Panticosa.

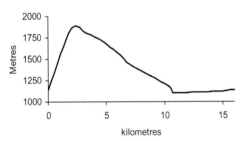

FORMIGAL SKI STATION

There are plans to open two lifts to bikers in the summer months though whether or not this will occur may depend upon this area remaining a candidate for the winter Olympics 2010.

The GR 11 is a well-marked route that criss-crosses the ski slopes. It is possible to pick this up from the main A136 road just before the turning to Formigal and just before the roadside km marker of 95, the GR 11 starts on your left. The locals recommend taking this GR route up through the centre of the ski slopes. Following the markers to Os Sarrios where the last lift goes up to Collado de Izas at 2200m. About a third of the way up this last lift it is possible to go between the big peak on your right Lapazuso (2147m) and the long spur on your left Las Negras de Izas (2200-2300). As you pass Lapazuso there is another peak in front of you called Campo de Troya (2224) at the base of which you can pick up the SVT (Sendero Valle de Tena). There is then a long marked path that is a red BTT Fuera de Pista route downhill back towards the main road just above Formigal.

VALLE DE TENA **RIDES**

Ride 4: Embalse de Escarra

⬌ **5km**

⧗ **¼ day**

Leave Escarilla on the main road going uphill towards the tunnel. As you leave town, take the first road on your left before you reach the tunnel. Where there is a small signpost to Sandinies turn right off the road onto a vehicle track going uphill. Follow the GR route as it heads towards Embalse de Escarra. Zigzag uphill passing through two gates. At the third gate is a signpost on your right marking the start of the PR HU 91 back to Escarilla. Take this technical singletrack descent back to town. Watch for walkers.

ACCOMMODATION

The range of Accommodation and restaurants are extensive with a hint of French tastes and styles creeping across the border, indeed most Spaniards seem to speak French in one form or another.

Formigal
H**** Hotel Villa de Sallent, 974 490 223.
H*** Eguzki Lore, 974 490 123.
H** Tirol, 974 490 377.

Sallent de Gállego
H*** Bocalé, 974 488 555.
H** Almud, 974 488 366.
H* Balaitus, 974 488 059.
Hs** Centro, 974 488 019.

Escarrilla
H** Mingo, 974 487 223.
H** Ibon Azul, 974 487 211.
Hs* Sarao 974 487 065.
Camping Escarra 1.a C., 974 487 154.

Panticosa
H*** Sabocos, 974 487 488.
H** Morlans, 974 487 057.
H* Panticosa, 974 487 000.

METEOROLOGICAL INFORMATION FOR THE AREA IS FOUND AT WWW.GENCAT.ES/SERVMET

OTHER AREAS TO EXPLORE

Val d'Aran is relatively close by. Hop over into France and check out what their ski resorts have on offer. Printed on the readily available Editorial Pirineo map series there are some recommended bike routes. These are extensive and challenging. The GR 11, 15 and 16 run through this area and are always worth exploring. It is worth having a look at the ride below the Osseau glacier on the GR11 in the Valle del Ara.

PICOS DE EUROPA

PICOS DE EUROPA
CANTABRIA

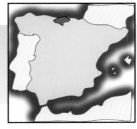

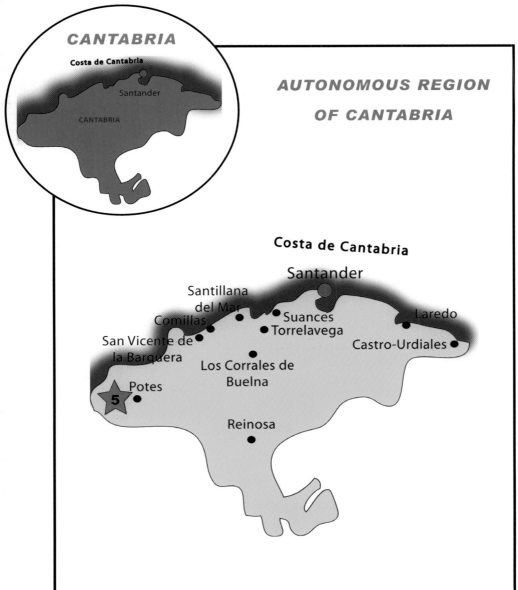

CANTABRIA

Costa de Cantabria

Santander

CANTABRIA

AUTONOMOUS REGION

OF CANTABRIA

Costa de Cantabria

Santander

Santillana
del Mar

Comillas

Suances

Torrelavega

Laredo

San Vicente de
la Barquera

Castro-Urdiales

Los Corrales de
Buelna

5 Potes

Reinosa

PICOS DE EUROPA
NORTHERN SPAIN

Location

Potes is conveniently located just over 100km from the ferry port at Santander making it one of the closest destinations for British riders. The village is situated in the Río Deva River valley. This watercourse twists down a particularly attractive and narrow gorge called the Desfiladero de la Hermida but the only access road (N621) is crammed into this thin ravine along side the river. Driving to Potes is therefore slow going and long traffic jams accumulate at the weekends and peak summer season. The harsh weather and inaccessibility means the higher villages are particularly isolated. The buildings are striking and reminiscent of Shakespearean England made of black beams and white wattle and daub walls. These ramshackle structures vividly sag from centuries of trying to stay upright.

General Background

The Picos de Europa are a beautiful set of mountains condensed into a relatively small area. The whole range is just 40km east to west and 25km north to south but, within this restricted space, the land rises up to great heights and contorts itself into some beguiling shapes and sizes. Whether you see it when it is sunny, misty, snowy, cloudy, rainy, stormy, there is always an intriguing vista being created by the inexhaustible natural palette of colours. Modern businesses thrive on outdoor activity enthusiasts and there are guides for every conceivable extreme sport.

The Weather

The weather is extremely changeable as Atlantic fronts move in swiftly. The mountains regularly attract clouds to their summits and a sunny day can quickly cloud over and vice versa. Thick fog and all types of precipitation are common place. The winters are very harsh and the higher mountains are not really visited by anyone other than hardcore ice climbers and skiers. The area mostly shuts down in October and reopens in spring.

Protected Status

The National Park Picos de Europa was created in 1995 and now covers 647km^2 including three massifs: Macizo Ándara, Macizo El Crornion and Macizo Central/Macizo Los Urrieles. Despite being protected countryside, there are few restrictions and the only place where riding is prohibited is the excellent trail that follows the river in the Cares gorge. This is specifically closed to mountain bikers.

Local Dangers

Although there are a wolves and bears in the area you are very unlikely to encounter them. The real danger here is the weather. The speed with which it changes is frightening and lives are regularly lost. Taking water, food and warm clothes is essential and easy to forget whilst you prepare for a ride in the warmth of the valley. Have a clear idea of your route and tell someone where you are going and when to expect you back. Always take good waterproof gear even on hot days. Although the rainfall is abundant, water courses have gone underground and there are surprisingly few places to find water so take plenty with you.

Mountain Range
Picos de Europa, Cordillera Cantábrica.

Highest Peak
Torre de Cerredo 2648m.

Getting There
✈ Madrid (300km).
⊙ Oviedo (140km).

Nearest Town/City
Potes/Torrelavega (90km).

Equipment Type
XC

Recommended Bases
Potes.

Tourist Information
Calle Independencia, Potes 39570, Tel 942 730 787.
National Park Office, Casa Dago Avenida de Covadonga, 43, Cangas de Onis, 985 848 614.

Ride Guides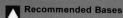
Europicos, San Roque 6, Potes. www.europicos.com,
Pedal Picos www.pedalpicos.com 0207 813 0296.

Body Repair
Potes Hospital 942 730 102.

MISTY, MYSTICAL AND
MONUMENTALLY STEEP, THESE
MOUNTAINS MAKE FOR SOME
MEMORABLE RIDING

☑ Equipment

Light, fast bikes are essential because the gradients are so steep. It is imperative that your gears are working well and your chain is strong. You will be spending considerable time in your granny ring. Always carry good weatherproof clothing in your backpack; take equipment that anticipates sudden changes in weather.

XC Cross-Country

Steep uphill sections and fast, wide descents are the most common type of riding and finding good rides is easy amongst the abundant vehicle tracks cutting through the mountains around Potes. There is an insanely tough ascent into the mountains from Espinama. Masses of 4x4's use it to ascend towards Sotres.

FR Freeride

It can be worth exploring the PR S15 from Fuente De and the PR S7 from Pido to Cosgaya. The singletrack rides we describe are hard to follow and littered with patches of large head sized boulders. Freeride bikes can cope with these steep, technical descents but a day's riding in the Picos can be hard work on a heavy bike. If you want sweet singletrack you are going to have to push it in more ways than one!

DH Downhill

A cable car takes you from Fuente Dé up the mountain. The lift rises dramatically from 1080m to 1850m in just 1.15km to the top of the Macizo Central cliff face. Provided you are one of the first in the queue you can take a bike. To beat the coach loads of visitors you need to be at the ticket office before 9.00 a.m. when it opens (Tel. 942 736 610). It is closed in January and February or when the weather is rough. There is therefore the scope for taking a heavy bouncy bike up the mountain and trying some adventurous descents. The only problem is you need to think about how you will return to your vehicle if you leave it at the cable car station. As an alternative to the cable car there are many companies that arrange 4x4 shuttles up the mountain they go up the PR S2 from Espinama.

Much of the singletrack riding is hard to follow making it easy to get lost and the gradients are incredibly steep and long. However, since most of the best riding centres around the Río Deva valley, if you do get lost you can always head down into the valley and pick up the N 621 road that runs alongside the river between Potes and Fuente Dé. Potes is a good central location to radiate from because, as well as good riding, the town is well serviced by shops, bars and restaurants.

Maps ☺
Series: Mapa Topográfico Nacional De España, 1:25,000 81-I (31-11) and Potes 81-II (32-11); Editorial Alpina 1:40,000, Parque Nacional Picos de Europa Macizo Central Y Oriental. Buy in Potes.

Banks ☺
Potes.

Fuel ☺
Ojedo.

Bike Repair ☹
Garaje Liebana S.C. Potes, 942 730 220. A garage with a section for basic bike bits.

Bike Hire ☺
Europicos, San Roque 6, Potes www.europicos.com.

Other Activities
Climbing, potholing, horse riding, canoeing, hiking, canyoning, caving, paragliding, quad biking, 4 x 4 excursions, cross country skiing.

Day Off
Sample some Cantabrian cuisine, local blue cheese (queso de Cabrales), cured meats and cider are highly prized. Walk the Cares Gorge. Visit the lakes at Covadonga.

Best Riding Times

J F M A M J J A S O N D

PICOS DE EUROPA **RIDES**

Ride1: Fuente Dé Cable Car

⬌ **20km**

⧗ **½ day**

🍴 ▨

💧 ▨

⬜ ☺

GPS points

N	W
1. *N43 09 213*	*W004 46 274*

Take the cable car from the village of Fuente Dé. At the top ascend for 1.25km to the first major junction where you ignore the left turn. Turn right following the PR S 2/16 to the Refugio Hotel Odriozola de Aliva. From the hotel follow the vehicle track that descends in front of the bar terrace. After a 2km descent you join a track coming from the left from a church called 'Virgen De Las Nieves'. Turn right away from the church. After 1.6km you reach a fork (GPS 1). Go left and ascend for 500m to a gate. 500m from the gate turn left uphill at a fork. Stay on the vehicle track for about 7km descending to the village of Mogrovejo. You come out at a church. Turn right to the village. Follow the road downhill to you meet the N621. On the far side of the road is a downhill trail to Camaleño.

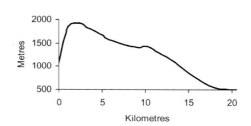

Ride 2: Espinama Ascent

⬌ **20km**

⧗ **¾ day**

🍴 ■

💧 ▨

⬜ ☹

GPS points

N	W
1. *N43 09 213*	*W004 46 274*
2. *N43 08 887*	*W004 44 619*
3. *N43 08 138*	*W004 44 018*
4. *N43 07 433*	*W004 44 146*
5. *N43 07 110*	*W004 43 906*

From Espinama take the very well used PR S2 vehicle track from the middle of town. Climb a gruelling 4km passing through a deserted old town of Invernales de Igüedri until you reach a cattle grid. Turn right just after this cattle grid (GPS 1). After 500m uphill you go through a gate. After 500m ignore the right going downhill and continue left uphill. At the next major junction go right heading for Llaves (GPS 2). At the next junction go right. Exactly 880m from this junction turn right onto a singletrack that is very hard to spot (GPS 3). To find it, look right when the gradient of the track you are on becomes particularly pronounced. Also wooden fences and Llaves village comes into view as you approach the turn. Turn right onto this singletrack and follow it for about 1.4km until you reach the church at Pembes. Turn right and go more or less straight through the village for 250m until you join a vehicle track at the back of the village. Go left at the first junction. About 500m further ignore the right turn and descend on small trails to a grassy area at (GPS 4) where the trail seems to end. It resumes a few metres downhill and to the right. After 1km from here you join a vehicle track. Go left downhill (GPS 5) and you come out behind the Hotel Del Oso. Go right on the main road back to Espinama.

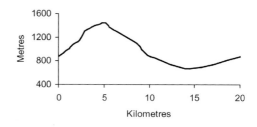

A DAY SPENT TOPPING UP ON
TAPAS AND TASTING THE LOCAL
TREATS CAN BE A PLEASANT
WAY TO WHILE AWAY TIME

Ride 3: Pembes Path

↔ **20km**

⧗ **¾ day**

🍸 ■

💧 ▦

▣ ☹

GPS points

N	W
1. *N43 09 248*	*W004 40 894*
2. *N43 08 870*	*W004 41 799*
3. *N43 08 720*	*W004 42 108*
4. *N43 08 057*	*W004 42 960*
5. *N43 07 110*	*W004 43 906*
6. *N43 07 433*	*W004 44 146*
7. *N43 07 797*	*W004 45 666*
8. *N43 08 159*	*W004 43 730*
9. *N43 08 292*	*W004 43 268*

From the San Pelayo Campsite (GPS 1) turn right on the N621 main road away towards Camaleño. After 1.35km you reach Camaleño. Turn left immediately before the main road crosses the river. Follow the track on the left bank of the river for 600m to a three-way junction. Take the track on the left (GPS 2). After 700m go right at a junction (GPS 3). After 1.3km rejoin the main road and turn left. Follow the road straight for 600m until it goes around a left-hand bend. On this bend turn left off the road onto a path going steeply uphill (GPS 4). After 750m go straight over a crossroads. 1.3km further on you meet a tarmac road. Go right downhill for 500m until you rejoin the N 621 main road. A road sign says 6.5km Espinama and 13km Potes. Go left for 240m to the small town of Areños and cross the little bridge and cycle behind the Hotel Del Oso. Follow the trail steeply uphill to a sharp left-hand bend where a singletrack begins on your right (GPS 5). Turn onto this. After 1km the trail seems to end at an open grassy area. The trail resumes a few metres uphill (GPS 6). After 1km there is a fork. Go left. After 500m is another junction, go right and follow the trail into the village of Pembes. Go more or less straight through town bearing slightly to the right until you reach the church on the far side (GPS 7). Immediately after the church is a grass track on your left. Take it. After about 700m is a fork, turn right uphill. After 500 m ignore a right turn. 100m further join a wider vehicle track. Go downhill to Llaves. Again go through town and find the church on the far side of town (GPS 8). Go past the church on the concrete road and continue to a fork by two pylons/masts. Turn right downhill past the two masts (GPS 9). At the first junction go right. Descend to a house about 900m from the radio masts. 50m past the house is a large galvanised pole; turn right down a small path. At the first fork go left. After 500m downhill you join a road. Go left uphill to the village of Mogrovejo. Go through town passing a bar and church and go downhill to Redo village. Bear right when you get to the village and join a vehicle track. This track goes downhill then up to meet a road going to Tanarrio. Follow the road downhill. At the first right hand bend turn left onto a small path signed PR S7 and 8 back to San Pelayo. This is a 1km long singletrack that takes you back to the campsite.

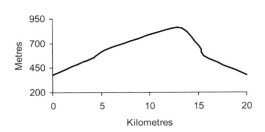

Metres (y-axis): 950, 700, 450, 200

Kilometres (x-axis): 0, 5, 10, 15, 20

PICOS DE EUROPA RIDES

Ride 4: Camaleño

↔ **12.5km**

⧗ **¼ day**

Ψ ▮

⬤ ▮

▣ ☺

GPS points

N	W
1. *N43 08 057*	*W004 42 960*
2. *N43 08 870*	*W004 41 799*

Starting in Areños follow the main road towards Potes passing in front of the Hotel Del Oso. After about 200m turn right where there is a road sign showing 6.5km to Espinama and 13km to Potes. Go up hill on this minor road for about 500m and turn left onto a vehicle track behind a property. Follow the path downhill for about 1.4km on this track to a crossroads. Go straight over for 700m and drop onto the main road (GPS 1). Go right on the main road for about 600m until you reach a bar on your left and a road going up to Mogrovejo. Follow the small track on the right and descend to Camaleño (GPS 2). Follow the main road back to the start.

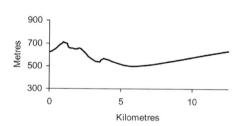

YOU CAN OBTAIN WEATHER UPDATES FROM: WWW.ABC.ES/TIEMPO/PRECISION/ESP/PRECISION9.HTML.

Ride 5: Ermita De San Tirso

↔ **25km**

⧗ **1 day**

Ψ ▮

⬤ ▮

▣ ☺

Start on the C627 road out of Potes passing through Frama after 2.3km. 6km from Potes turn left to Torices. 4km uphill you reach Torices. 175m into town ignore the track going south-west to your right. Climb through town and the road becomes a vehicle track. Pass above a private swimming pool to your right. About 500m from here you reach two gates. Go left and the trail becomes thinner and views open up to the north. Follow the trail for about 500m where there is a choice of two tracks; turn right onto the lower one. Follow the track for 1.7km to a barbed wire 'gate'. 3.5km further on you reach Som Aniezo. Find the track between here and Luriezo. It begins on the west side of Som Aniezo and crosses a small bridge just as you leave town. After 1.8km there is another bridge on a sharp left hand bend. From Luriezo follow the GR 71 road for 2.6km to Cahecho. Follow the red and white markers of the GR 71 route back to Ojedo. 1.6km from Cahecho is a firebreak and major junction of about 5 routes. Go east downhill on the GR 71. About 1.6km from this junction you pass the Ermita De San Tirso on your right. A little further on and you descend on some rocky switchbacks frequented by quad bikes.

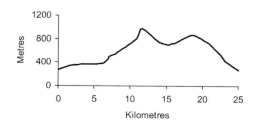

ACCOMMODATION

The campsites usually shut for winter in September/October and reopen in spring. Most of the accommodation that is open during winter will only be on skeleton crew.

Potes
Casa Cayo, 19, Calle Cantabra 6, Potes, 942 730 150, fax 942 730 119.
***Hotel Valdecoro Calle Roscabao 5, Potes, 942 730 025.
**Restaurante El Fogón De Cus, Potes, 942730 060.
*Hostal Lombraña Calle del Sol 2, 942 730 519.
*Favila, Potes, Tel. 942 738 018.

Camping san Pelayo, Baro, 942 730 896 (closes in September).
Camping La Isla, 942 730 896.
Camping La Viorna, Near Potes, 942 732 021.

Tama
Casa Gustavo Guesthouse, Tama, 942 732 010 www.holidaybank.co.uk/canfab.

Camaleño
***Jisu, Camaleño, 942 733 038.

Fuente Dé
***Parador Río Deva, Fuente Dé, 942 736 651.

OTHER AREAS TO EXPLORE

There are some good routes to explore in the Cares River Valley. The main town to head for is Arenas de Cabrales. If you drive through Poncebos and on to Sotres there are some good tracks between Sotres and Beges. It is possible to ride between the Cares and Deva River Valleys but extremely hard work.

The 12km uphill route to the lakes at Covadonga is a mecca for uphill junkies.

Central Spain

SIERRA DE GREDOS

SIERRA DE GREDOS
ÁVILA - CASTILLA-Y-LEÓN

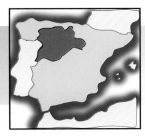

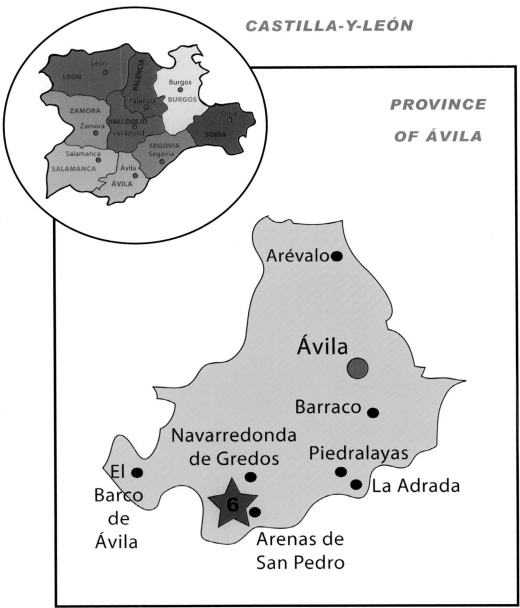

CASTILLA-Y-LEÓN

PROVINCE

OF ÁVILA

León
LEÓN
PALENCIA
Burgos
Palencia
BURGOS
ZAMORA
Soria
Zamora
VALLDOLID
Valladolid
SORIA
Salamanca
SEGOVIA
Segovia
SALAMANCA
Ávila
ÁVILA

Arévalo

Ávila

Barraco

Navarredonda
de Gredos
Piedralayas

El
Barco
de
Ávila
6
La Adrada

Arenas de
San Pedro

THE GRANITE AND STEEP
ELEVATIONS CHANNEL WATER
OFF THE MOUNTAINS AND
CREATE MANY NATURAL SPRINGS

SIERRA DE GREDOS

CENTRAL SPAIN

Location

The Sierra de Gredos falls within the four provinces of Madrid, Ávila, Caceres and Salamanca. The town that is the focus for this riding area is called Arenas de San Pedro and it is about 110km due east of Madrid.

Unusually for Spain, these mountains are predominantly granite rock; most of Spain's mountain ranges are limestone. The existing mountains were created 40 million years ago at the start of the alpine orogeny. Glaciers shaped the range (approximately 4 million years ago) giving classically smooth glaciated features to the landscape including smooth U-shaped valleys and lakes such as the "Laguna Grande de Gredos" and "Las Cinqo Lagunas". The end result is a set of attractive mountains that have a slightly unusual appearance compared to the rest of the Nation's landscape.

General Background

The area has a strong history of human presence. Most prevalent are the Roman remains found in abundance. There is an impressive pass through the mountains called the Sierra Del Pico on the N502 main road just North of Arenas de San Pedro. An ancient Roman road is being reconstructed through this pass and it is worth visiting. This is not a major tourist spot. It is a pretty regular provincial Spanish town and this makes it intriguing because it is a side of Spain foreign visitors do not usually experience. As a consequence, English is not spoken by many. An understanding of Spanish is important.

The Weather

This is a spring and autumn destination only because summer is so hot and winter brings heavy snow and freezing temperatures. The major wet periods are between February and March and November and December.

Protected Status

These hills are protected as a regional park. This means that recreational activities such as cycling are permitted so long as they do not deteriorate the environment or endanger other park users. You are not permitted to stray from existing paths but, if a footpath exists, you can ride it.

Local Dangers

Although most of the springs produce the purest water you are likely to drink, a couple of springs have become contaminated. There are no warning signs but the spring below El Arenal was infected with hepatitis. If you drink

---

Mountain Range
Cordillera Central, Sierra de Gredos.

Highest Peak
Almanzor (2592m).

Getting There
✈ Madrid (180km).
🚌 Ávila (75km).

Nearest Town/City
Arenas de San Pedro/Ávila (75km).

Equipment Type

Recommended Bases
XC FR

Arenas de San Pedro, El Hornillo, El Arenal, Guisando.

Tourist Information
Arenas de San Pedro tourist office, 920 370 005,
www.ayto-arenas.com & www.guiatietar.com.

Ride Guides
Meet up with the friendly locals on Sunday mornings in front of the bike shop Freebike, Arenas de San Pedro.

Body Repair
MedicoEmergencies, 920 370 221.
Ambulances, 920 386 169.
Red Cross, 920 371 466.

ASCEND ON VEHICLE TRACKS
AS FAR AS YOU ARE ABLE AND
THEN ENJOY THE EXCELLENT
SINGLETRACK DESCENTS

from springs above towns the water will be fine. Some of these sources dry up during the summer. The dense forests are home to many species of wild animals and this attracts many hunters. They are quick on the draw and it is worth wearing bright colours to distinguish yourself from wild game to ensure you aren't shot at!

☑ Equipment

Bouncy bikes just aren't needed for these soft forest floors. Speed and lightness will serve you better than weight and travel. There are very technical descents to be found but they are short lived and few and far between.

DH Downhill

The downhill options are limited in the rolling undulations of the forests but it can be worth looking at some of the wide fire breaks. They are easy to spot and follow.

XC FR Cross-Country and Freeride

The summer fires, harsh winter snow and constant felling of trees by the forest management means trails get swallowed up and altered regularly. This makes it an ideal location for cross-country riders who have the desire to explore and don't mind getting lost. The wide vehicle tracks are permanent features and kept well used by forest management teams, hunters and the fire brigade.

👁 Local Observations

From Arenas de San Pedro there emanates a network of tracks through the forests. The long wooded tracks are easy to find and follow. The difficulty here is finding and following good technical singletrack. Refuel at their understated but excellent bar/restaurants - check out the steaks served in the restaurant near the campsite at Guisando. The locals rate the riding around the peak of La Penca (north east of El Arenal).

Maps 😊
Series: Mapa Topográfico Nacional De Espanna, (578-I) El Arenal and (578-III) Arenas De San Pedro 1:25,000. Buy in book shops in Arenas de San Pedro.

Banks 😐
Arenas de San Pedro.

Fuel 😐
Arenas de San Pedro.

Bike Repair 😊
Freebike, Avenida de la Constitucion, 8. Arenas de S.P.

Bike Hire 😞

Other Activities
Horse riding, rock climbing, canoeing, hiking. 2 night clubs. Winter: cross country skiing.

Day Off
Go to the Sierra Del Pico pass on the N 502 just North of Arenas and explore the reconstructed Roman road and take in the views from top. Visit the impressive walled city of Ávila. Madrid is accessible from this location.

Best Riding Times

J F M A M J J A S O N D

SIERRA DE GREDOS RIDES

Ride 1: The Cerro de Las Cabezas Ridge and La Penca

⬌ 27km

⧗ ¾ day

GPS points

N	W
1. N40 16 021	W005 04 639
2. N40 15 076	W005 04 877
3. N40 14 993	W005 04 731
4. N40 17 137	W005 03 397
5. N40 17 267	W005 03 671

Start at the town of El Arenal. Head south east out of town on the main road towards Mombeltran. Follow the signs for the Campo de Futbol. 1km from town pass a playground on the right (GPS 1). 800m from here pass the Campo de Futbol (football ground) on your right. Continue on the road for 1.9km until you reach a sharp left-hand bend in the road. Turn left up a steep concrete track (GPS 2. after 100m turn right following a vehicle track past a small house with a pool to your right. Immediately after the house turn right onto a singletrack descent (GPS 3). Follow this trail south for 1 km until it joins the main road. (This section of trail is on the border between two maps - 578 I and 578 III). Turn left on the road (you soon pass a spring on the left). After 1.7km turn left onto the Camino de Moranega. Follow this for 2.3km then turn left at a junction. Continue for 900m and turn right. Stay on this track until you reach a spring called the Fuente Larga (GPS 4) where you meet the main road. Turn left on the road ascending the switchbacks for 1.1km to the Collado de la Centenera Mountain pass (GPS 5). Turn left off the main road before it begins to descend. Climb the steep vehicle track and, at the top, follow the firebreak along the ridge of Cerro de Las Cabezas to the south to La Penca. Just after the summit of La Penca turn left onto the vehicle track going in an easterly direction. After 1.8 km you rejoin the forest track that you ascended earlier. Turn right on this for 800m going through three major bends. At the next junction turn right. Continue straight on until you rejoin the main road then turn right to return to El Arenal.

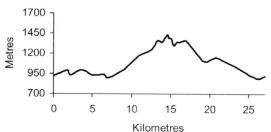

Ride 2: Puerto de la Cabrilla

⬌ variable

⧗ variable

From El Arenal take the main road going north climbing above town signed for Puerto la Cabrilla and the town swimming pool/piscina. After just over 1km turn left on the road signed to Puerto de La Cabrilla that heads towards a campsite (that's closed). Take the second right off this road again following signposts for Puerto de la Carbrilla. Follow this vehicle track. Look out for the green topped wooden posts marking out a footpath. Take the first vehicle track on your right going steeply uphill. Ascend on the vehicle track as far as you are able to. As you ascend look for a singletrack cutting across the switch-backs in the vehicle track you are ascending on, it is marked with posts. Follow these markers downhill to enjoy an excellent singletrack descent.

Ride 3: Arenas de San Pedro to Guisando Circuit

↔ **21km**

⧗ **½ day**

GPS points

N	W
1. **N40 12 729**	**W005 05 976**
2. **N40 12 749**	**W005 07 120**
3. **N40 13 188**	**W005 07 498**
4. **N40 13 798**	**W005 06 294**
5. **N40 14 753**	**W005 07 326**
6. **N40 14.932**	**W005 06 591**
7. **N40 14 807**	**W005 06 027**

Start from the small car park in front of the castle in Arenas de San Pedro. Take the main road to Guisando. 750m from Arenas, just before you reach the reservoir called Embalse de Riocuevas on your right, turn left onto the vehicle track called the Camino Forestal Del Lancharon (GPS 1). Climb steeply for 800m then bear right. Follow the main track as it turns to the left 90m further on. Ascend until you go through an olive grove. At the next junction by a fenced in property (GPS 2) ignore the left downhill and go past the building continuing on to Collado de Guadyerbas. Rejoin the main road to Guisando (GPS 3) after a total climb of about 3.5km from Arenas de San Pedro. Turn left on the road passing the spring Fuente Anita on your right and continue for 1.3km to Guisando. At Guisando turn right at the fork in the road ascending steeply into the village. 600m from the fork turn right and head for the Refugio El Hoyuelo. The tarmac road comes to a dead end at the Refugio (GPS 4). With the Refugio behind you turn right and head north on a vehicle track for 2.1km to a T-junction. Turn left. Immediately after you come to a junction by a small Refugio. Take the vehicle track that passes to the right of this small building. 75m beyond it is a left turn onto singletrack (GPS 5). Descend all the way to the main road and turn right for 400m to a picnic site called Las Escarilluelas where there is a spring (GPS 6). The singletrack descent resumes opposite the spring. Descend to the village of El Hornillo and you come out by the bridge at the bottom of town. Follow the main road away from town and almost immediately turn right up the steep road going to Guisando. After 300m turn left and go downhill (GPS 7) for just under 2km to the main road. Turn right on the road and after 100m turn left just before the Campamento El Tejar. Continue south downhill all the way back to Arenas de San Pedro.

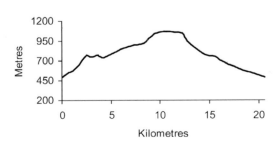

Metres / 1200 950 700 450 200 / 0 5 10 15 20 / Kilometres

SIERRA DE GREDOS RIDES

Ride 4: Nogal del Barranco

↔ **18km**

⧗ **½ day**

Y ▮

◆ ▮

⬚ ☹

GPS points

N	W
1. N40 12 729	W005 05 976
2. N40 12 749	W005 07 120
3. N40 13 188	W005 07 498
4. N40 13 629	W005 09 319
5. N40 13 000	W005 08 502

Start from the small car park in front of the castle in Arenas de San Pedro. Take the main road to Guisando. After 750m turn left before you reach the reservoir - Embalse de Riocuevas (GPS 1). Follow the Camino Forestal Del Lancharon Climb steeply up this vehicle track. After 800m bear right then left 90m further on. Climb through an olive grove to a property with a fence around it (GPS 2). Ignore the left downhill and continue past this building until the track rejoins the main road to Guisando (GPS 3). Continue on the main road to Guisando and turn right at the fork at the town so you climb steeply into the village. After 1.3km ignore the road going to the left to the camp site and continue straight on towards the Refugio and monument at Nogal Del Barranco. After 1.7km from the last junction look to the left of the road and find the obscure footpath (GPS 4) that begins 400m before the Campamento Luis Manuel Lopez - a Spanish Scout Camp. Descend on this trail. At the first fork turn right and then immediately left. You come out on the main road. Turn right going past the entrance to the Campsite Los Galayos. Cross the bridge. At the next junction turn right uphill. After 1.3km find the obscure singletrack dropping steeply down to your left (GPS 5). Descend to the main road. Join the vehicle track that descends past Guisando's football ground. This eventually ends at the N 501 main road. Go straight over the main road and follow the vehicle track with the main road on your left back to Arenas de San Pedro.

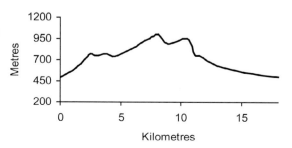

THIS IS A SPRING AND AUTUMN
DESTINATION ONLY BECAUSE
SUMMER IS STUPIDLY HOT AND
WINTER BITTERLY COLD

Ride 5 : The Palacio de Los Borbones

🔄 **21km**

⌛ **¾ day**

🍽 ◼

⛽ ◼

🏁 ☹

GPS points

N	W
1. *N40 15 664*	*W005 04 761*
2. *N40 15 076*	*W005 04 877*
3. *N40 15 945*	*W005 02 614*
4. *N40 14 284*	*W005 03 860*

From the Palacio de Los Borbones (a well known, small palace on the edge of Arenas de San Pedro) there is a well ridden forest track (pista forestal) going due north up to the Campo de Football ground just outside El Arenal 7km away. Follow this track. After 4.4km you pass the Collado de la Cruz de la Tendera. After 7km you reach the football ground (GPS 1). Join the main road just beyond it and turn right heading away from El Arena. After 1.9km at a sharp left hand bend in the road turn left onto the steep concrete road (GPS 2). Ignore the first right after 100 m and continue for 1.7km where you turn right at the Collado Del Portezuelo. Continue for 2.5km to the next obvious junction and turn right (GPS 3). After 1.4km you come to a cross roads with the main road. Go straight over and continue for a short way on a vehicle track. At the next junction turn right going downhill south west towards the Monasterio de San Pedro de Alcantara. 2.5km from the main road turn right at a junction (GPS 4) where the trail becomes singletrack. It ends at a tarmac road going to the Monastery. Turn left on this road to return to Arenas.

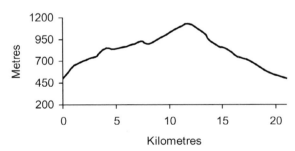

SIERRA DE GREDOS RIDES

Ride 6: Campamento El Tejar via the Embalse de Riocuevas

↔ **12km**

⧗ **¼ day**

🍸 ▮

💧 ▮

⛶ ☺

GPS points

N	W
1. *N40 13 798*	*W005 06 294*
2. *N40 14 062*	*W005 06 098*
3. *N40 14 807*	*W005 06 027*

From Arenas de San Pedro follow the main road towards Guisando until you reach the reservoir - Embalse de Riocuevas. Take the track anti-clockwise around the edge of the water. Half way round the reservoir turn right away from the water uphill on a wide earth track and follow it to the road just outside of El Hornillo. About 1.9km from the reservoir is a 90° switch back and some big granite horizontal rocks. At the junction after this turn left (GPS 1). Continue climbing up to the road just south of El Hornillo (GPS 2). Turn right onto the road and follow it for 1.7km. Just after passing a concrete road to the left turn right (GPS 3). Follow it downhill to the next main road. Turn right on this for 100m then left going past the Campamento El Tejar. Continue south all the way back to Arenas de San Pedro.

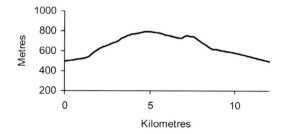

OTHER AREAS TO EXPLORE

If you head over to the pass called the Sierra Del Pico on the N 502 just North of Arenas there is a reconstructed Roman road that you are allowed to ride down. There are plenty of worthwhile rides nearby to explore. This location is not a long way from San Lorenzo de El Escorial and Manzanares El Real. There is plenty of good riding concentrated around the Sierra de Guadarrama which are the hills at the far end of the Cordillera Central.

ACCOMMODATION

Accommodation is hard to come by in this area. It is not frequented by international tourism and there are few hotels. There are some charming guest house type places to stay and good mountain campsites.

Camping Riocantos, Camino Ceavientos, s/n, 920 372 547.

Guisando
Camping Los Galayos, Guisando, 920 374 021.

Arenal de San Pedro
Hostal Isabel, Calle de las Angustias, 920 375 148.
Hostal/Restaurante El Castillo, Ctra de Candeleda 2, 920 370 091.
Hosteria Los Galayos, Plaza de Condestable Davalos 2, 920 371 379.
Casa rural Las Gesillas, Ctra de Candeleda, Km.5, 600, 920 370 818.

La Fuente
Posada rural El Canchal, La Fuente, 920 37 09 58.

Ramacastañas
Hostal/Restaurante Las Chuletas, Ctra Grutas Del Águila 1, 920 37 08 85.

LA PEDRIZA NATURAL PARK

SIERRA DE LA PEDRIZA
COMUNIDAD DE MADRID

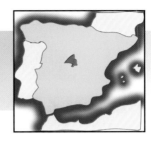

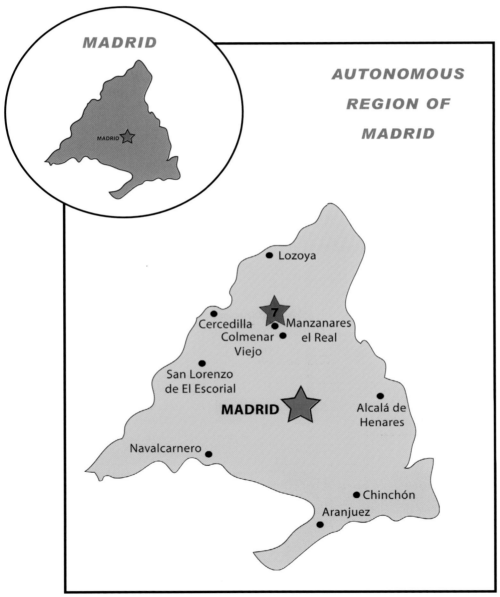

MADRID

MADRID

AUTONOMOUS REGION OF MADRID

Lozoya

7

Cercedilla
Colmenar
Viejo

Manzanares
el Real

San Lorenzo
de El Escorial

MADRID

Alcalá de
Henares

Navalcarnero

Chinchón

Aranjuez

LA PEDRIZA NATURAL PARK

CENTRAL SPAIN

Location

The focus of this area is the Pedriza Mountains in the north of the Regional Park De La Cuenca Alta Del Manzanares. Just outside of the town of Manzanares El Real you find a visitor centre at the entrance to the La Pedriza Park. The riding all takes place from here. The whole area was initially declared a reserve in 1930 because of the spectacular geological formations. Ever since it has gained in recognition and size so that it now extends for 46,728 ha. all the way to the edge of Madrid. In Manzanares El Real there is a quaint 15th century castle - 'Castillo de Los Mendoza'. There is a good supermarket, an adventure shop with a good but expensive range of maps and a number of bars and restaurants.

General Background

The intriguing rock formations of the La Pedriza Mountains are the main attraction to this area. The geological processes that created this landscape are complex. Granite plutons were intruded in the Hercynian Orogeny and then thrust up into horst/grabens during the alpine mountain building phase. Over time the granite has been significantly eroded and exposed leaving a stunning landscape particularly favoured by rock climbers.

The Weather

From October to May rainfall is consistently high but in summer it drops off dramatically and temperatures quickly rise. After this brief heat wave, the area usually experiences a dramatic cooling off from November through to March when the average temperature is about 80C. There is therefore a concentrated period during the summer when the area is best to visit.

Protected Status

The entrance to the Regional Park is 'guarded' by an information centre. Riding on vehicle tracks is unrestricted; however, the park authorities had a mixed response when asked about bikers using footpaths. Off road riding is not specifically prohibited on singletrack but it seems to be discouraged. You should seek advice before attempting our suggested rides.

Local Dangers

The weekends are a time to avoid. All natural spaces around Madrid become a playground for the active Madrileños who escape the city in hordes. There are often long queues to enter the park.

Equipment

There is no need for big travel or heavy bikes. Hard tails and light cross-country bikes are good but if you intend to check out the riding at San Lorenzo de El Escorial,

⌂ **Mountain Range**
Sierra de Guadarrama, Sierra de La Pedriza.

Highest Peak
Cabezas de Hierro (2383m).

Getting There
✈ Madrid (50km).
🚃 Soto Del Real (5km).

Nearest Town/City
Manzanares /Madrid (50km).

☑ **Equipment Type**
XC FR

▲ **Recommended Bases**
Manzanares El Real.

ⓘ **Tourist Information**
Centro de Educación Ambiental, at the park entrance.

✝ **Ride Guides**
Puerto de Navacerrada, Deporte y Montana, Calle de Sagasta 13, Madrid, www.puertonavacerrada.com.

Body Repair
Mountain rescue GERA, 609 254 712 & 639 569 081.

A VALLEY DESIGNED FOR
VELOCITY WITH EASY
CLIMBS TO STAGGERING
HEIGHTS AND VAST VISTAS

PROS + CONS
+ Easy to follow rides
+ Close to other riding areas
+ Impressive singletrack
+ Close to Madrid
− Small riding area
− Singletrack riding can be discouraged

something more robust would be good to have to hand.
If using light tyres, carry a spare with you.

Cross-Country

There is a major forest track creating a spine road through these hills (ride
2). It is very popular with cross-country riders and the circuit is in constant
use during the weekends. It is particularly special because it allows riders
to climb to a staggering height (1700m) with little danger of getting lost.

DH Downhill

None of note.

FR Freeride

The popularity of walking and climbing means there is a network of
singletrack throughout the woodland. Unfortunately the rocky
outcrops mean many of these trails are impassable to mountain bikes
because they are too technical; only hikers can penetrate them. Having
said that, if you have time and a map it is worth hunting around for
trails that might be passable because those that can be ridden are
exhilarating. There is an incredibly long and technical piece of
singletrack that starts to the south east of the Maliciosa Baja peak
(ride 3). Check with the authorities before riding it.

◉ Local Observations

Beware the weekends when the area becomes saturated with city slickers from Madrid. There are regularly
queues into the park. There has been the danger of poisonous water in the rivers. Check the current situation
with the local information office. There are trails filling the hillsides between the Embalse de Santillana
reservoir in the south and the Cabeza de Hierro peak in the north of the mountains. This is an exceptional but
limited riding area where vultures are the indisputable kings of the skies. Fortunately the park is very close to
San Lorenzo de El Escorial and Cercedilla where there is ample riding to bolster the lack of trails in this park.

Maps ☺
Series: La Pedriza Del Manzanares, Parque Regional de
la Cuenca Alta Del Manzanares, 1:15,000. Buy in the
climbing shop called El Refugio in Manzanares El
Real, La Tienda Verde, Maudes, 23 - 28, Madrid,
www.tiendaverde.org.

Banks ☺
Manzanares. Soto Del Real.

Fuel ☺
Manzanares. Soto Del Real.

Bike Hire ☹

Bike Repair ☹
See section on Sierra de Guadarrama for closest shops
(San Lorenzo de el Escorial and Madrid).

Other Activities
Rock climbing, hiking, bird watching & fishing.

Day Off
Visit the Monastery at San Lorenzo de El Escorial or
Franco's mausoleum close by at Vale de Los Caidos. Also
ideally suited for a day trip to Madrid.

**Best Riding
Times**

J F M A M J J A S O N D

LA PEDRIZA RIDES

Ride 1: The PR M1 up and GR10 down

↔ **14km**

⏳ **½ day**

🍴 ▮

💧 ◼

⬚ 😐

GPS points

N	W
1. **N40 45 010**	**W003 53 657**
2. **N40 45 813**	**W003 53 570**
3. **N40 45 753**	**W003 53 169**

Start at the Centro de Interpretación (Information Centre) at the entrance to the Parque de la Pedriza. This is little more than a kilometre west of Manzanares El Real. Go through the barrier at the entrance to the park and follow the main road through the park for 4km until you reach the Canto Corchino car park where there are two café/bars and a Casa Forrestal nearby. Go through the car park to the river at the bottom. Cross the bridge over the river (GPS 1) and turn left following the yellow and white markers for the PR C/M 1 route. Initially there are a lot of painted markers because of the sheer number of junctions making it easy to get lost. Ensure you follow the markers to stay on the right path. After a few hundred metres the path becomes clearer as the number of paths reduces. The trail climbs gently at first becoming steeper and steeper. Follow the markers for about 2km from the bridge until the climb ends at an enormous boulder (GPS 2). There is a yellow and white marker painted on this rock in the shape of a right angle indicating the PR route goes around to the left. Ignore this left turn and turn right leaving the PR route. Immediately there is a three-way junction. Take the middle route that descends steeply zig-zagging downhill. Descend for about ¾km to a T-junction with the PR 2 and GR 10 routes (GPS 3). Turn right and follow the GR red and white markers for about 1.6km back to the bridge. Return the way you came. Watch for singletrack options on either side of the main road as you descend back to the information centre.

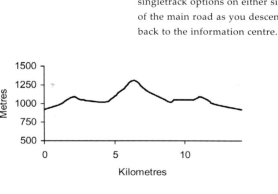

SPIN THROUGH SPECTACULAR
GEOLOGICAL FORMATIONS THAT
SUPPLY SINGULARLY STUNNING
SCENERY AND SINGLETRACK

Ride 2: Collado de Los Pastores

 37km

 ¾ day

GPS points

N	W
1. N40 45 076	W003 53 812
2. N40 45 520	W003 55 594
3. N40 46 091	W003 55 596
4. N40 46 299	W003 54 560

This ride can be done backwards or forwards. It does a circuit of the massive vehicle track that skirts the edges of the Pedriza Park's boundaries. Start at the Centro de Interpretación (Information Centre) at the entrance to the park and follow the main road for 4km until you reach the Canto Corchino car park (GPS 1). Continue 300m past this parking area until you reach a fork in the road. Turn left uphill going around the traffic barrier at the start of this road. Ascend for about 2.75km to the first major right hand bend where there is a vehicle track on the apex of this turn. Bear right onto this forest track (GPS 2). Continue for 1.7km to the next major switch back (GPS 3). Continue for 2.6km to another major bend. Climb for 2.6km from here to the next major bend. 800m beyond this and you reach the summit of a ridge called Collado de Los Pastores where there is an information area with information boards. Continue for 850m and you cross a small stream. There is a short descent followed by yet more ascending. Eventually you begin to zig-zag steeply downhill through pine woods until you descend to a river - the Rio Manzanares. Cross over the bridge (GPS 4) and continue for 3.6km keeping the river on your left until you return to the Canto Corchino car park. Continue back to the start.

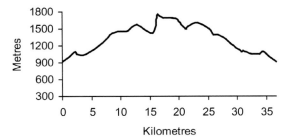

LA PEDRIZA RIDES

Ride 3: Canto Corchino Circuit

↔ **23km**

⧗ **¾ day**

GPS points

	N	W
1.	N40 40 076	W003 53 812
2.	N40 45 520	W003 55 594
3.	N40 46 091	W003 55 596
4.	N40 45 556	W003 56 284
5.	N40 45 692	W003 56 480
6.	N40 45 350	W003 55 357
7.	N40 45 259	W003 55 330

Start at the Centro de Interpretación (Information Centre) at the entrance to the park and follow the main road for 4km until you reach the Canto Corchino car park on your right (GPS 1). Continue past this for 300m until you reach a fork in the road. Turn left uphill going around the barrier to stop traffic. Ascend for 2.75km until you reach the first major right hand turn that is on the corner of a switch-back in the track you are on. Turn right onto this forest track (GPS 2). Continue for 1.7km to the next major switch-back (GPS 3). Continue on the main track ignoring the right turn. After 1.6km look to your left for the start of some singletrack and note its position (GPS 4), as you will be descending on it later. Continue on the main track for 1km to another major switch-back. Climb for a further 1.55km from this bend and look for the start of a singletrack beginning on your right (GPS 5). It is obscure but marked by two rocks. The start is steep and tricky to negotiate. Descend for 600m until you reach the vehicle track you originally ascended. Cross over it (going slightly to the right) onto the singletrack noted earlier (GPS 4). Descend for 1.5km until the singletrack comes to a natural end on a vehicle track. There is a big stack of rocks opposite (GPS 6). Turn right on the road and after about 120 m there is a square concrete drainage construction on your left where the singletrack resumes (GPS 7). Descend for a further 2¼km until you return to the road opposite the Canto Corchino car park. Return the way you came in.

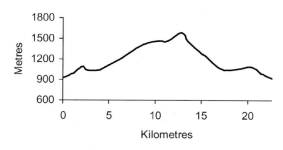

ACCOMMODATION

There is a campsite at Manzanares but it really caters for the weekend influx from Madrid. It often closes in winter but if you turn up during a quiet season they are quite amenable to letting you stay.

Hostal El Tranco, Calle Del Tranco 4, 918 530 063;
Camping Manzanares El Real.

OVER TIME THE GRANITE HAS BEEN
ERODED AND EXPOSED LEAVING
A STUNNING LANDSCAPE
FAVOURED BY ROCK CLIMBERS

OTHER AREAS TO EXPLORE

The Cuerda Larga/Cuerda Castellana is a rideable, extensive
forest track taking in 55 peaks between the Puerto de Somosierra
to the north and the Puerto de la Cruz Verde in the south west.
San Lorenzo de El Escorial is nearby offering great riding.
Cercedilla is even closer where a train can take you and your
bike up to Puerto de Los Cotos. There are long descents back
into Cercedilla from there. For information email
redcentrosfuenfria@hotmail.com.

SIERRA DE GUADARRAMA

SIERRA DE GUADARRAMA
COMUNIDAD DE MADRID

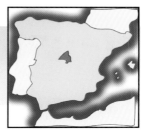

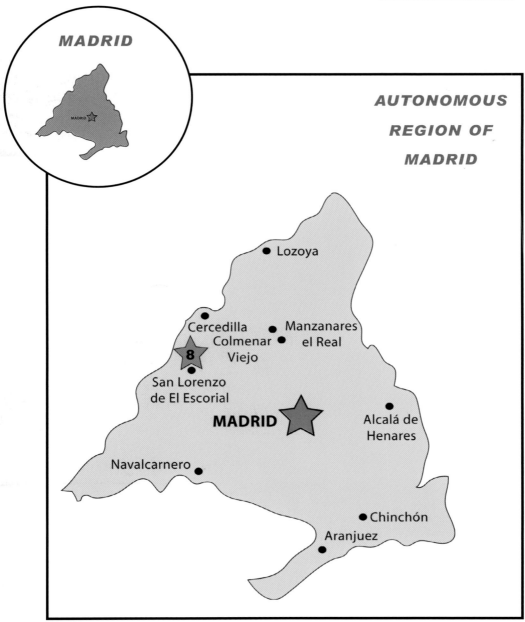

MADRID

AUTONOMOUS
REGION OF
MADRID

● Lozoya

● Cercedilla
Colmenar ● Manzanares
Viejo   el Real

8
●
San Lorenzo
de El Escorial

MADRID ★

● Alcalá de
Henares

Navalcarnero ●

● Chinchón
Aranjuez ●

SIERRA DE GUADARRAMA

CENTRAL SPAIN

Location

Madrid is founded on the flat central plains of central Spain known as La Meseta. It is a landscape that is typically comprised of undulating, arable farmland. At San Lorenzo De El Escorial all this changes. The flat scenery gives way to the Sierra de Guadarrama Mountain Chain that rises impressively out of the plains. San Lorenzo De El Escorial is a small town nestling under the first looming peak of these mountains - The Abantos Mountain. This peak practically rises straight out of the back walls of the last buildings in town. The town's location makes it an enchanting place and this has long been recognised by the affluent, aristocratic Spanish and it has been particularly favoured as a royal retreat. Although only 50km from Madrid, the town feels like it is a lifetime away from this bustling cosmopolitan capital.

General Background

For centuries this city was the summer court for Spanish Monarchs. Although San Lorenzo De El Escorial is only the size of a modest town, it is classified as a city because of the construction of an enormous monastery built by King Philip II after his victory over King of France in the Battle of San Quintin. This impressive structure has been increasingly improved over time and is a testament to Spain's might during the 16th century. It gradually became a seat of learning and there still exists a renowned library. The overall splendour of this structure is dazzling. Any building that has an 'Ante-Chamber of Eternity' and a Church with 43 altars is deserving of respect. It is therefore unsurprising that the city is recognised by UNESCO as a Monument of World Interest.

The Weather

Madrid and its environs are situated on the flat central plains of Spain. The weather in this area is notorious for being freezing in winter and scorching in summer. Nestled as it is at the foot of protective mountains, the steep walls of the Sierra de Guadarrama protect it from the harsh northerly weather systems in the winter and provide cooler conditions in the summer. It is therefore pleasantly hot in summer and relatively tolerable in winter.

Protected Status

There are a couple of fenced in areas that are farmland or protected zones but these are clearly no go areas. On the whole, riding is acceptable anywhere in the mountains.

Local Dangers

Although the town is well protected from the elements by the mountains, the riding is all found much higher up and is therefore exposed to harsher conditions. It is usual for cloud to cling to the summit of the mountains making losing your bearings a particular concern. The descents are rocky and can often be wet adding to the danger.

Mountain Range
Sierra de Guadarrama.

Highest Peak
Abantos 1753m.

Getting There
Madrid (50km).
San Lorenzo De El Escorial.

Nearest Town/City
San Lorenzo De El Escorial/Madrid (50km).

Equipment Type
XC

Recommended Bases
San Lorenzo de El Escorial.

Tourist Information
Oficina local , C Grimaldi 2, Tel 918 905 313.
Tourist office San Lorenzo De El Escorial, c
Floridablanca, 10, Tel 918 901 554.

Ride Guides
As you would expect to find in Spain's capital, a really professionally organised bike club sponsored by Specialised. Club Mammoth: www.mammoth-mtb.com, C/Fuente Del Berro 9, 28009 Madrid, 913 093 259.

Body Repair
Red Cross, 918 904 141
Hospital San Lorenzo De El Escorial, 918 973 000.

THE AREA WILL SUIT TOUGH
RIDERS WITH TOUGH KIT WHO
ARE JUST AS STRONG GOING UP
AS THEY ARE COMING DOWN

PROS + CONS

+ Teaming with technical trails
+ On Madrid's doorstep
+ Geographically sheltered

- Tough climbs on all rides

☑ Equipment

There is a good range of different types of rides so there is no ideal
choice of bike. As a general rule, the rocky terrain tends to favour
more heavy-duty equipment, strong tyres and good gears. A
waterproof should never be out of your backpack.

XC Cross-Country

Once you have overcome the steep southern slopes of the Abantos
Mountain, the terrain at the top becomes more undulating and there are
plenty of routes that spread out across the ridges high above San Lorenzo
De El Escorial. Especially good vehicle track routes can be seen snaking
off towards Robledondo from the 'Puerto de Malagon' mountain pass.

FR Freeride

The rocky, steep slopes above San Lorenzo make this a free-ride heaven.
The GR 10 provides an easy to follow ribbon of quality singletrack that
undulates along the ridge of the mountains towards Franco's tomb. For
something steeper, the southern slopes of the Abantos Mountain are
packed with a network of steep, technical challenges.

DH Downhill

The drover's path called the Cañada Real is used for downhill
competitions. You can get a blurry view of the flat plains towards
Madrid as you hurtle downward from 1600m to 1000m in moments.

👁 Local Observations

Any mountainous area close to Madrid is bound to attract interest from riders regardless of trail quality. However the
appeal of San Lorenzo De El Escorial is not just a consequence of it being the only hilly area in an otherwise flat region.
The quality of these trails cannot be overstated. Local riders are talented and the abundant riding is exploited by both
on- and off-road biking events. Festi Bike is a particularly famous annual event with competitions and expositions. The
varied trails provide a wide spectrum of riding suiting most styles. The best trails focus around the Abantos Peak.

🗺 Maps ☺
Series: Comunidad de Madrid Hoja 6, San Lorenzo De
El Escorial, 1:50,000. Buy in La Tienda Verde, Maudes,
23 - 28, Madrid, 915 330 791, www.tiendaverde.org.

💲 Banks ☺
San Lorenzo de El Escorial.

🛢 Fuel ☺
San Lorenzo de El Escorial.

✖ Bike Repair ☺
See last page for bike shop listings.

🚲 Bike Hire ☹
Racing Components San Lorenzo de El Escorial, Pozas
36-38 local 17, Aptdo 198, 918 905 897..

👉 Other Activities
Rock-climbing, hiking, skiing, hunting, fishing, horse
riding, quad-biking, motor cross riding.

⛰ Day Off
Visit the Monastery because it is so spectacular both
inside and out. Another monument is that of Franco's
mausoleum. He is buried in the Valle de Los Caidos.
Accessing Madrid from this area is easy. Go.

⚙ Best Riding Times

J F M A M J J A S O N D

EL ESCORIAL RIDES

General Access for the Rides

↔ **11km**

⧗ **2 hours**

Y ▢

🌢 ▢

▣ ☺

GPS points

	N	W
1.	**N40 36 616**	**W004 07 787**
2.	**N40 36 610**	**W004 08 344**
3.	**N40 35 966**	**W004 09 312**

For the start of most rides, you need to climb the small mountain road that goes up to the 'Puerto De Malagon' mountain pass (1554m). This pass is near the top of the Abantos Mountain. From this vantage point you overlook San Lorenzo De El Escorial. The climb is a minor road found off the M600 main road just outside of San Lorenzo De El Escorial. There is a café at the entrance to the turning. To find it, head from Guadarrama towards San Lorenz De El Escorial on the M600. Just outside of San Lorenzo De El Escorial there is a major roundabout. The minor road is found 400m before this roundabout on the right. As you turn up this road past the café, you enter a wooded area where there are picnic facilities. It can be safer to go around the roundabout and double back rather than crossing the fast road. Look for singletrack and dirt jumps in the woods.

To ascend to the mountain pass - 'Puerto de Malagon', climb the small road for 700m from the M600 road and café until you pass a vehicle track on your right that goes into a field. Ignore this. 500m beyond it, turn right onto a major vehicle track with a barrier across it (GPS 1). Climb steeply for 2km going through about 10 sharp switchbacks until the track levels out and goes into some woods (GPS 2). Follow it for 2.5km on a fairly level gradient until you rejoin the road at a barrier (GPS 3). Turn right on the road and follow it uphill for a further 4.6km until the steep road ascent ends and you arrive at the pass at the top of the mountain.

THE APPEAL OF SAN LORENZO DE EL ESCORIAL IS
NOT JUST A CONSEQUENCE OF IT BEING THE
ONLY HILLY AREA IN AN OTHERWISE FLAT REGION;
THE QUALITY OF THE TRAILS IS EXCEPTIONAL

Ride 1: Technical GR Route

↔ **25km**

⧗ **½ day**

GPS points

N	W
1. N40 36 623	W004 10 359
2. N40 36 937	W004 09 363
3. N40 36 818	W004 09 291
4. N40 36 843	W004 09 410
5. N40 36 442	W004 09 622

Ascend to the Puerto de Malagon pass near the Abantos Mountain Peak. When the road stops ascending, it turns right and traverses the ridge on top of the mountain. On this bend there are a number of vehicle tracks, one going left and uphill (towards Robledondo) and one going straight down to a reservoir (Embalse De El Tobar). Ignore these. Stay on the main road for 800m from the pass until a vehicle track appears on your right (GPS 1). Leave the road and follow this track for 1.8km towards the Abantos Peak until you come to a cattle grid (GPS 2). Continue for about 270m beyond the cattle grid then turn right onto a barely discernible path going down into the woods (GPS 3). You are heading for a stone font-type construction about 70m below the track into the trees. From this stone font, continue 100m downhill, down the centre of a grassy slope. At the bottom find the clearly defined rocky path (part of the GR 10) (GPS 4). Descend on this rocky route for 600m until you see a finger of rocks forming a ridge ahead of you. Follow the (very technical) trail as it descends more steeply to the left of this ridge into dense forest (GPS 5). Various paths traverse the mountain. They all end by meeting the main road far below. Many carry on over the road. Either use the road or find a trail to get back to town.

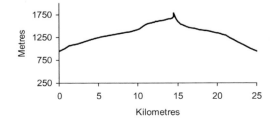

EL ESCORIAL **RIDES**

Ride 2: Cañada Real Downhill Route.

↔ **7km**

⧗ **½ day**

GPS points

N	W
1. **N40 36 227**	**W004 10 382**
2. **N40 36 013**	**W004 10 239**
3. **N40 35 801**	**W004 09 884**
4. **N40 35 782**	**W004 09 540**

A descent called the Cañada Real begins From the Puerto de Malagon. Start at the pass at the top of the mountain where the road turns to the right and there is a junction with various vehicle tracks, as mentioned in Ride 1. With these vehicle tracks behind you, go 30m downhill on the road back towards San Lorenzo de El Escorial. After this short distance, turn right off the road (GPS 1) onto the Cañada Real - an obvious scar in the earth going practically straight down cutting through the bends in the road so that you repeatedly cross and re-cross the tarmac. The first crossing is about 200m from the pass (GPS 2). Continue across the road until you again cross the road lower down (GPS 3). The trail eventually ends at a sandy vehicle track cutting from left to right across the Cañada Real path (GPS 4). Turn left on this track and follow it until you come to a fence. Go along beside the fence, slightly uphill, to the road. Use the road to return to the start of the ride.

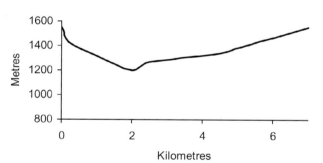

Ride 3: Abantos Peak

14km

½ day

GPS points

	N	W
1.	N40 36 623	W004 10 359
2.	N40 36 937	W004 09 363
3.	N40 36 989	W004 09 071
4.	N40 37 214	W004 09 558
5.	N40 37 414	W004 09 680
6.	N40 38 199	W004 10 244
7.	N40 37 824	W004 10 758

As with rides 1 & 2, start at the top of the Abantos Mountain where the main road stops ascending at the Puerto de Malagon pass. Follow the main road to the right. Continue on it for 800m then turn right onto a vehicle track (GPS 1) as in Ride 1. After 1.8km you reach a cattle grid (GPS 2). Turn left immediately before this and ascend the GR 10. After a tough climb of about 1km you reach the summit of the Abantos mountain (1753m) where there is a white metal cross and weather station (GPS 3). From here the GR 10 follows a wall just behind the weather station. It is an easy to follow ribbon of trail travelling along the ridge of the mountains in a north westerly direction. Follow it keeping the wall to your right. Go straight through the first two crossroads you come to at (GPS 4) and (GPS 5). At the second one you have to go through a small gate, ignoring the large gate to your right. Continue until the trail descends through a wood. This becomes increasingly rockier. You eventually reach a Refugio stocked with wood (GPS 6). Leave the GR 10 at this point. To do so, stand in the entrance to the building and face away from it. Head directly away from the entrance on an obvious path. There is a very rocky descent. Continue for just over 1km until the trail joins the main road (GPS 7). Turn left on the road and follow it for about 2km until you cross a cattle grid on the county boundary just beyond which there is a large sign indicating the province 'Castilla Y Leon De Avila'. Continue on the road for another 1.8km back to the start.

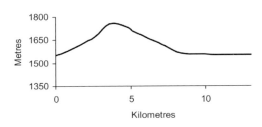

EL ESCORIAL RIDES

Ride 4: Embalse de la Acena

15km

½ day

GPS points

N	W
1. N40 36 623	W004 10 359
2. N40 37 277	W004 10 760
3. N40 37 082	W004 11 572
4. N40 37 034	W004 12 782
5. N40 37 767	W004 11 358

From the Puerto de Malagon pass, follow the main road north as in the other rides. After 800m ignore the vehicle track on your right (GPS 1) used in rides 1 & 3. Continue on the road for 1km until you cross a cattle grid. Just beyond this you cross the county boundary, marked by a large 'Castilla Y Leon Provincia De Avila' sign. 500m from the cattle grid is a lay-by on the left (GPS 2). Turn into this and follow the vehicle track that descends at 90° degrees to the road taking you towards the big reservoir 'Embalse de la Acena' in the valley below. After 1.25km from the road you reach a gate in a wall (GPS 3). Instead of going through the gate, leave the vehicle track and follow the small path running down the right hand side of the wall. Follow this rocky singletrack for about 1.75km always keeping the wall to your left until the trail drops steeply away from the wall (GPS 4) into some woods. After about 100m downhill the trail splits. Turn right following a thin path through woodland and you soon drop onto a vehicle track going around the edge of the La Acena reservoir. Turn right on this track and follow it for about 2.7km to the main road. You come out by the Hostal Casa de la Cueva (GPS 5). Turn right on the road and follow it for 3.9km back to the start.

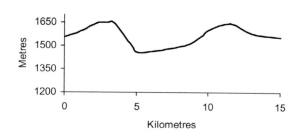

ACCOMODATION

San Lorenzo de El Escorial
Albergue El Escorial, Calle de la Residencia 14, 918 905 924.
Albergue Santa Maria Buen Aire, 918 903 604.
Hostal Vasco, Plaza de Santiago 11, 918 901 619.

Campsite El Escorial on the M 600 main road. One of the best sites in Spain with two enormous swimming pools, a large complex with restaurants, bars, shops and activities. Fixed caravans, bungalows and large open grassy areas for camping available. Camping Caravaning El Escorial, Crta de Guadarrama, M - 600, Madrid, Espana, 918 902 412, planeta.azul@mad.servicom.es.

BIKE SHOPS

SAN LORENZO DE EL ESCORIAL
Millan, Ventura Rodriguez, 7, San Lornezo De El Escorial, 890 15 82.
Racing Components SL Pozas 36-38 local 17, Aptdo 198, 28200 San Lorenzo De El Escorial, 918 905 897.

MADRID
Mammoth, c/Fuente Del Berro 9, 28009 Madrid, 913 093 259. Top quality shop.
Mammoth, C San Joaquin 6, 28220 Majadahonda, 916 341 788.
Ciclos Delicias, Po de Las Delicias, 65 Bis, 28045 Madrid, 915 307 787.

OTHER AREAS TO EXPLORE

Towards **Peguerinos** and Valle de Los Caidos/Franco's tomb there are plenty of long vehicle tracks and minor roads to explore.

Very close by is the **Natural Park of La Pedriza** at Manzanares El Real (see Page 90). This has some incredible single track riding.

The Sierra Guadarrama
During the summer you can access a plethora of beautiful mountain trails some of which join up with the GR10.1. Take the train from Cercedilla up to Puerto de los Cotos (1830m) and ride back via Puerto de Navacerrada, down hill all the way. In winter the area is a minor ski resort with minimum facilities. Cercedilla is the best base camp.
www.puertonavacerrada.com.

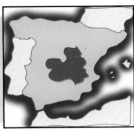

SERRANÍA DE CUENCA
CUENCA -
CASTILLA-LA MANCHA

CASTILLA- LA MANCHA

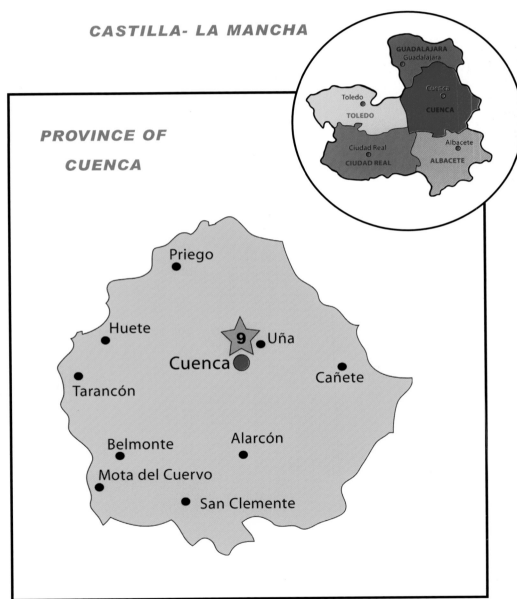

PROVINCE OF
CUENCA

SERRANÍA DE CUENCA
EASTERN SPAIN

Location

The City of Cuenca is found mid way between the Mediterranean coast and Madrid lying in the south-western foothills of the Serranía de Cuenca Mountains. This is the first high ground to break the flat central plateau of inland Spain. It is a fairly wet region making it an oasis amidst arid surroundings. The landscape away from the city is equally inspirational. The beautiful Júcar River valley to the North between Cuenca and Uña contains the best riding. The province of Cuenca is divided into 3; Sierra, Alcarria and Mancha. Alcarria is the arid part with the Sierra section being our main focus. The Mancha area is home to the world famous Manchego cheese and is dotted with windmills and castles.

General Background

The old town crammed on top of the steep sides of an impressive gorge was initially constructed by the Moors. The houses come right up to the edges of the cliffs where the walls of the city literally melt into the rock faces. The organic way in which these dwellings morph into the rocks like Escher drawings is fascinating and led to Cuenca becoming named a UNESCO World Heritage City. These 'hanging houses' are known locally as 'Casas Colgadas' and are progressively becoming internationally famous. Interesting rock formations are abundant but the 'Enchanted City' (Ciudad Encantada) in particular is home to the most curious of the natural limestone sculptures. Centuries of fluvial erosion have left these whimsical karstic characters which have been given names and legends by the Spanish. Neolithic cave paintings and Roman Settlements indicate early human activity but Cuenca rose to its zenith in the 16th century when the textile industry was thriving. This industry declined in the 17th Century and the region is barely recovering from the economic downturn. Tourism is the driving force behind the modern economy and with good reason; it is a beautiful place to visit.

The Weather

The area receives a great deal more precipitation than its neighbours. It can be wet and cold with snow falling as early as October. The temperature range is between 37°C and -6°C.

Protected Status

Riding is permitted in all areas except for the protected zone of the Ciudad Encantada. The only other fenced off areas tend to be places where there are dangerous drops into gorges.

Local Dangers

The weathered mountains are indicative of the harsh elements. Although beautiful they are inhospitable. Exposure to the elements is a serious danger.
Once you are out in the wilderness you are on your own as there are few places to stop and take shelter so you should be well prepared for outdoor life.

Mountain Range
Sistema Ibérico, Serranía de Cuenca

Highest Peak
1550m Cabeza de la Herrada.

Getting There
✈ Madrid (164km); Alicante (327km).
🚉 Cuenca.

Nearest Town/City
Villalba de la Sierra/*Cuenca*

Equipment Type
XC

Recommended Bases
Villalba de la Sierra.

Tourist Information
Glorieta González Palencia, 2, 969 178 843.
Infotur Office, 969 232 119 near old centre at Plaza Mayor. www.cuenca.org.

Ride Guides
None.

Body Repair
Medical emergency, 969 230 131.
Hospital de la Virgen, 969 224 211.

THE WALLS OF THE GORGE
MORPH INTO THE OUTER WALLS
OF THE BUILDINGS TO CREATE THE
FAMOUS 'HANGING HOUSES'

PROS + CONS
+ Well drained, forested riding
+ Beautiful rock formations
+ Endless, easy to find trails
+ Peaceful
− Often wet and stormy
− Under developed

☑ Equipment

Lightweight full suspension bikes are best suited to the long and laborious uphills and hard, rocky surfaces. Heavy, bouncy bikes are cumbersome because of the distances you need to cover. Whilst semi-slicks would be good for covering ground quickly, they are soon worked to the bone. However, wide tyres will be a noticeable drag on the long rides; choose something in between. Some form of lighting is essential for the ride along the river below the Devil's Window. A well equipped back pack with clothing and supplies is crucial.

XC Cross-Country

The area is most suited to cross country riding. Riders who like a blend of long fast, flowing tracks punctuated with occasional technical drops will enjoy this area.

FR DH Freeride and Downhill

The best downhill in the area is the GR route near the Ciudad Encantada that goes downhill from the Mirador de Uña and ends at the Village of Uña. There is also a good, if short lived, drop down into the Júcar River gorge opposite the junction of the CM2105 and 2104. The subsequent ride along the river is only for those who have a torch or are not afraid of the dark!

👁 Local Observations

All of the best rides seem to be to the north of Cuenca where there is an abundance of woodland dissected by long vehicle tracks. The bulk of the riding is found off the main road (CM2105) between Cuenca and Uña and the CM 2104 road that leads to the Enchanted City. Footpaths and singletracks are often too steep for even the most talented riders, however, the sections of singletrack that are negotiable are phenomenal grin generators that will have you smiling into your cerveza. Whether summer or winter, conditions are rough. Rides tend to be long, gradients steep and the rocks hard so you need to be prepared for endurance riding.

📍 Maps 🙂
Mapa Topográfico Nacional de España, 1:25,000,
1. Villalba de la Sierra, 587 - III; 2. Uña, 587 - IV; 3.Las Majadas, 587 - II (48-45). Shop: Ministerio de Fomento.

💲 Banks 🙂
Cuenca.

💧 Fuel 😐
Cuenca.

✖ Bike Repair 😐
Ciclos Garcia, Fermin Caballero 7, Cuenca, 969 225 211. Nissan Main Dealer, Miguel Angel Villar Vila, Cervantes 15, 16004 Cuenca, 969 224 957.

🚲 Bike Hire 😞

👍 Other Activities
Hunting and fishing services (969 178 300), hiking, quad biking, horse riding, canoeing, absailing, canyoning, golf, health spas 'Balnearios' such as Solan de Cabras in the town of the same name.

📤 Day Off
Site seeing around Plaza Mayor, Cuenca. Visit the Enchanted City - Ciudad Encantada. Swim in the natural pools and spas found locally.

⚙ Best Riding Times

J F M A M J J A S O N D

CUENCA RIDES

Ride 1: Ventana del Diablo

13km

¼ day

GPS points

N	W
1. N40 13 796	W002 05 508
2. N40 14 573	W002 02 195

From the hotel 'Hostal Bayo' in Villalba de la Sierra (GPS 1) follow the CM 2105 main road towards Uña. After a few hundred metres you cross the river 'Rio Júcar'. Follow the road until you pass the Ventano Del Diablo lay-by after 1.8km. Continue for about another 4km to the top of the road climb where there is a right turn onto the CM 2104, which goes to the Ciudad Encantada. 550m before you reach this junction turn left off the main road (GPS 2) into a lay-by where a vehicle track descends steeply towards the river Júcar far below. Go right at each major junction heading downhill towards the river. At the bottom turn left onto the path along the bank of the river. Go through three tunnels only just wide enough to ride through. They are long and you must have some source of lighting to negotiate them. Eventually you come out beneath the Devils Window and the trail rejoins the main road. Follow it back to Villalba.

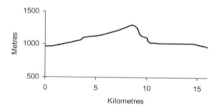

Ride 2: Uña to Majadas

25km

¾ day

GPS points

N	W
1. N40 13 451	W001 58 788
2. N40 15 507	W001 59 953
3. N40 15 600	W001 59 952
4. N40 16 571	W002 00 434
5. N40 16 663	W002 00 688
6. N40 17 708	W002 01 319

Start in Uña. Head out of town on the main CM 2105 towards Villalba for a short distance. You pass the Bar Zabalos. Take the first right after the bar (GPS 1) and head up this vehicle track for 400m until it crosses a bridge over a concrete canal. Turn left following the canal. After 2.3km ford a stream. Continue for about 6km from Uña until the vehicle track comes to a natural end at a valley floor strewn with bushes (GPS 2). Cross this flat, bushy valley floor. Although only about 200m across, it is hard to negotiate. When the vehicle track ends follow the little footpath downhill to the bottom of the hill. After about 80m it crosses a small stream. Continue winding through shrubs for about 160m and you should begin to climb up the other side. From here there begins a much more obvious singletrack path going almost due north (GPS 3). Ascend on this tough climb for about 800m. After a total ascent of 3.5km you pass a spring on the right (GPS 4) where the footpath you have been following turns into a vehicle track. Another track soon joins you (GPS 5). Continue on the major track for 2.2km passing an old ruin and golf course. Eventually you come out in Majadas village (GPS 6) by a big notice board saying 'Serrania Alta De Cuenca' and children's play area. Close by is the Bar Meson El Cerrillo. Return the way you came enjoying the excellent singletrack descent you have just climbed.

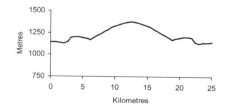

GRIN GENERATING
DESCENTS WILL HAVE YOU
SMILING AS YOUR SHOCKS
SOAK UP THE KNOCKS

Ride 3: Above Villalba

↔ **32km**

⧖ **1 day**

🍴 ■

🔥 ▪

⬚ ☹

GPS points

N	W
1. *N40 12 332*	*W001 59 377*
2. *N40 11 906*	*W001 59 543*
3. *N40 10 695*	*W001 58 712*
4. *N40 10 899*	*W001 59 944*
5. *N40 10 676*	*W002 00 403*
6. *N40 10 756*	*W002 01 463*
7. *N40 10 818*	*W002 02 127*
8. *N40 11 386*	*W002 02 830*
9. *N40 11 659*	*W002 03 027*

Follow ride 4 all the way to the Mirador de Uña. At the turning circle (GPS 1) ignore the GR route and continue on the vehicle track as it heads away from the viewpoint in a south-westerly direction. After 800m turn left at a junction (GPS 2). Essentially you head along the ridge overlooking Uña for 4km. At this point the track heads south, directly away from the ridge/cliff into a small, grassy valley. The trail becomes less obvious but follow the vehicle tyre marks around the edge of the grassy bank on your left. After 400m follow the vague route so that you almost do a U-turn to the left. After 400m you join a more pronounced track. Turn right onto this (GPS 3). Almost immediately the track goes through some switch backs up a small hill. After these bends the track flattens off. After 2.3km turn left at the junction (GPS 4). 350m further is a minor junction where you go right. 460m further is another small junction where again you go right. You soon come to an area cluttered with large and interesting rock formations (GPS 5). Look for a building on your right built into the rocks. Turn right here following the track for about 700m back to the CM 2104 main road (GPS 6). Go straight across continuing on the vehicle track on the other side for 1km to a fork. Turn right (GPS 7). 1.7km from the road a vehicle track joins from the left at a large rocky. Turn right here (GPS 8). Ignore 2 minor turn-offs and after 600m go left at a more pronounced junction (GPS 9). You undulate across a 'hogs back' type hill and from the top you can see Villalba in the valley below. Descend all the way on this track to a rough tarmac road at the bottom. Turn right and follow a long line of power cables eventually taking you back to Villalba.

Elevation profile: Metres (vertical axis: 500, 750, 1000, 1250, 1500) vs Kilometres (horizontal axis: 0, 5, 10, 15, 20, 25, 30)

CUENCA RIDES

Ride 4: Cuidad Encantada

⬄ 27km

⧗ ¾ day

GPS points

N	W
1. N40 13 796	W002 05 508
2. N40 13 847	W002 05 228
3. N40 13 412	W002 03 588
4. N40 13 388	W002 03 614
5. N40 13 353	W002 03 465
6. N40 13 317	W002 00 752
7. N40 12 332	W001 59 377
8. N40 12 753	W001 59 311
9. N40 12 957	W001 59 367
10. N40 13 462	W001 59 301

From the hotel 'Hostal Bayo' in Villalba de la Sierra (GPS 1) follow the CM 2105 main road towards Uña for a few hundred meters until it crosses the river 'Rio Júcar'. Take the first right (GPS 2) onto a minor road until it ends at a T-junction 400m from the main road. Turn left then right at the next T-junction after another 400m. Ascend steeply for 500m and ignore the first left turn. Continue for about 2km until the trail stops ascending. Eventually it descends through a series of 90 ° switch-backs to the valley floor; don't descend this far! The first switch-back bend is at GPS 3. 50m before this bend, turn right off the main track onto a very hard to locate footpath (GPS 4) marked by a small pile of stones/cairn. Follow it for 230m until it becomes a more pronounced vehicle track (GPS 5). Follow this increasingly obvious track uphill for 1.2km until it levels out and another trail joins from the right. Follow it for 3.5km to the CM2104 main road (GPS 6). Turn right following the main road to 'Ciudad Encantada'. Opposite the entrance to this tourist attraction is a large parking area and hotel/bar/restaurant on the left of the road. Turn into the car park and join the vehicle track at the back of this parking area and follow it in an easterly direction away from the 'Ciudad Encantada', passing a grey lookout tower and bank of solar panels after a short distance. After 1.5km you reach a turning circle and viewpoint looking to Uña. As you look over the this steep drop take the GR route descending to your left (GPS 7). After about 800m you come to a grassy section where there is a fork (GPS 8). Follow the GR markers to the left. After about 1.2km downhill the GR route meets a vehicle track (GPS 9). Turn left and follow the vehicle track back to the CM 2105 main road (about 1.5km) (GPS 10). To return to the start follow the CM2105 in a north west direction back to Villalba or stop at Uña for refreshments.

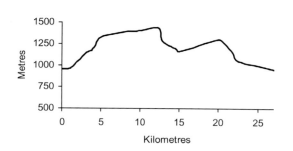

ACCOMMODATION

Cuenca
Camping Caravaning Cuenca, Ctra Cuenca Tragacete, km8, 16147 Cuenca, 969 231 656.
Parador de Cuenca, Paseo de La Hoz Del Huécar, s/n 16001 Cuenca, 969 232 320.

Alarcón
Parador de Alarcón, Ave Amigos De Los Castillos, 3, 16213 Alarcón, 969 330 316.

Villalba de la Sierra
Hostal-Restaurante Bayo, Villalba de la Sierra, Cuenca, 969 281 275.
El Tablazo, Camino La Noria, s/n 16140 Villalba de la Sierra, 969 281 488,
tablazo@canal21.es, tablazo@infonegocio.com, www.arrakis.es.

Valdecabras
Paraje Ciudad Encantada, Valdecabras 16192, 969 288 194.

OTHER AREAS TO EXPLORE

A relatively close area to visit is Albarracín for similarly remote rocky rides.

Eastern Spain

SIERRA DE ALBARRACÍN

&

MONTES UNIVERSALES

SIERRA DE ALBARRACÍN
TERUEL - ARAGÓN

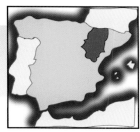

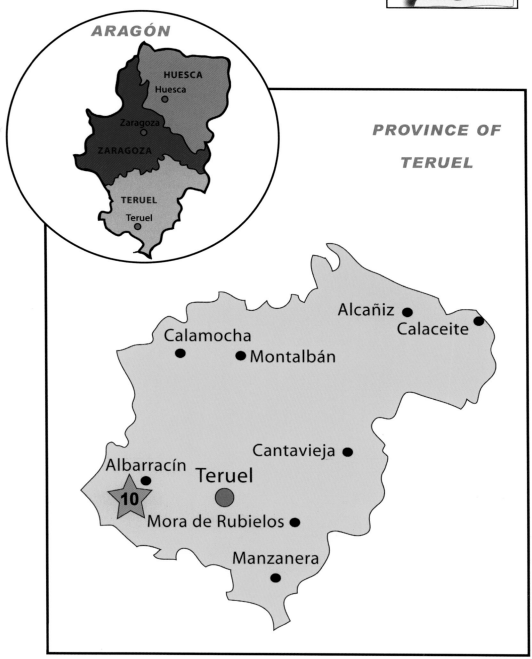

ARAGÓN

HUESCA
Huesca

Zaragoza

ZARAGOZA

TERUEL
Teruel

PROVINCE OF

TERUEL

Alcañiz

Calaceite

Calamocha

Montalbán

Cantavieja

Albarracín   Teruel

10

Mora de Rubielos

Manzanera

SIERRA DE ALBARRACÍN

EASTERN SPAIN

Location

The nearest city to Albarracín is Teruel. Travelling between the two reveals just how remote Albarracín is. It sits on a thin, flat plateau between two large mountain ranges: the Serrania de Cuenca and the Sistema Ibérico. The journey is well worth it, Albarracín is one of the most beautiful towns in the province. The medieval streets and ancient ironwork take you back in time. However, if Albarracín feels remote, travelling to Moscardón, Frías de Albarracín and Bezas will knock your socks off. These tiny villages are utterly removed from the pace of modern life. Each village literally consists of a handful of houses surrounding a bar. Hunting is usually the major pursuit. If you visit this area straight from a major city the peace and tranquil way of life will startle you. It is an unhurried, unknown corner of Spain with just the right kind of easy going riding to help you unwind. If you come from a cosmopolitan area, be prepared for a culture shock. This is a land where traditional values prevail.

General Background

Albarracín is a small citadel crammed onto a hilltop. An impressive fortress wall surrounds the old town. This defensive structure and the buildings within are all constructed from a rich red sandstone. Watching the countless shades of red that the buildings go through

before the sun finally sets each day is magical. This is a town with a very distinct character. Just a little outside of Albarracín the GR10 cuts through a protected area, the 'Paisaje Protegido de los Pinares de Rodeno'. Here you will find prehistoric rock paintings (pinturas rupestres). If it wasn't for these primitive diagrams, it would seem that this little town would be hidden from the world. Even with these remarkable paintings the area is only really visited by the Spanish. Geographic isolation keeps the region practically unknown to international tourism.

The Weather

Albarracín is built into a gorge in the mountains so that it shelters from the blustering winds that can race across the flat plains. Snow is a regular phenomenon during December, January and February and heavy rainfall can make it unpleasant riding during the winter months. Summer can be hot but shelter within the forests makes riding possible unlike the scorching southern provinces.

Protected Status

The Paisaje Protegido del Rodeno is the only protected area where you must stick to the tracks.

Local Dangers

The 4x4 tracks through the woods tend to split and rejoin. This makes following the ride directions tricky because there can appear to be more junctions on the actual trail than indicated in the instructions. These 'false junctions' can cause you to get lost and find yourself a long way from anywhere. Having a map with you is essential.

Mountain Range
Sistema Ibérico, Sierra de Albarracín & Montes Universales.

Highest Peak
1650m.

Getting There
Madrid (330km) and Alicante (346km).
Teruel (30km).

Nearest Town/City
Albarracín/Teruel (30km).

Equipment Type
XC

Recommended Bases
Albarracín.

Tourist Information
Old Town, Calle Diputacion No 4., Albarracín.
Calle de Tomas Nogues 1, 978 602 279.
www.albarracin.org.

Ride Guides
None.

Body Repair
Medico Centro Salud de Albarracín,
Camino del Cristo, 2, 978 710 127.
Red Cross, 978 710 062.

IF YOU VISIT THIS AREA
STRAIGHT FROM A MAJOR CITY
THE PEACE AND TRANQUIL
WAY OF LIFE WILL STARTLE YOU

PROS + CONS

+ Tranquil, deafeningly peaceful
+ Fast and endless tracks
+ Cheap and interesting accommodation
- Remote
- Little technical riding
- Limited infrastructure

☑ Equipment

Apart from the weathered sandstone in the gorge, most of the riding surfaces
are gravely/grassy vehicle tracks. Technical riding is virtually non existent so
most of the routes tend to require stamina. Hard-tails are the obvious choice
given some of the long climbs and long distances that need to be covered. You
always need to have a wind-cheater with you as you can be out for long
periods and when the winds pick up you can get a battering.

XC Cross-Country

The majority of the riding in the area is cross-country because of wide vehicle
tracks meandering through forests. Hills tend to be fairly gradual.

FR DH Freeride and Downhill

The best riding playground is found just outside of Albarracín around the caves.
The GR route that comes through the gorge following the stream Barranco
Cabrerizo is challenging at the top but a worthwhile test for bouncy bikes.

👁 Local Observations

Albarracín is the most beautiful and well-serviced town in the area making it the only viable place to stay. The smaller
villages don't have any shops. Apart from the GR singletrack through the gorge, much of the best riding is found
around Moscardón. To really kick back try a night at the inexpensive but superb Los Palacios restaurant/hostal.

The rides around Albarracín are largely dependent on the long
meandering 4 x 4 tracks created by off road vehicles. These
make the area extremely appealing for riders who like to cover
distances. This is not a destination for extreme riders but the
allure of the long, flowing rides that pass through woodland
and meadows is hard to deny. The low population means the
silence is deafening and this is an ideal rehabilitative venue for
stressed out executives who want to get away from it all.

🧭 Maps 😊
Series: Mapa Excursionista 1:40,000, 52 and 53 Serranía
de Albarracín, Montes Universales, Prames
Cartografía. Buy in Albarracín.

💰 Banks 😊
Off Plaza Mayor, Albarracín.

💧 Fuel 😊
Outskirts of Albarracín.

🔧 Bike Repair 😐
Acobis, Ciclos Mudejar, Pza. Merced no. 4, 44003,
Ciclos Mudejar, Pl Merced 4, Teruel, 978 610 445
Solo Bici, 978 612 371.

🚲 Bike Hire 😊
Acobis, Ciclos Mudejar, as previously.

👍 Other Activities
Climbing, hiking, horse riding, fishing, canoeing, quad
biking, hunting, 4x4.

🏔 Day Off
Visit the cave paintings just outside of Albarracín.
Take a day trip to Teruel and explore the impressive
Cathedral.

⚙ Best Riding Times

J F M A M J J A S O N D

ALBARRACÍN RIDES

Ride 1: Frias de Albarracin

↔ 16km

⧗ ½day

🍴 ▮

⛽ ▮

▣ 🙂

GPS points

N	W
1. *N40 20 105*	*W001 37 221*
2. *N40 18 892*	*W001 37 035*
3. *N40 18 256*	*W001 37 063*
4. *N40 18 188*	*W001 37 037*
5. *N40 18 130*	*W001 35 435*
6. *N40 18 179*	*W001 34 729*

From the bottom of Frías de Albarracín, leave town on the road going to Tragacete and Cuenca. Almost immediately pass a minor turn on the right by some ruins of a chapel. 300m from here turn left uphill onto a large vehicle track (GPS 1). Ignore all minor turn-offs. Pass a spring 2.6km from the road (GPS 2). Ignore a left turn 650m further on. Ascend steeply on the main track as it zigzags. At the summit stay on the major track ignoring a couple of minor turns. Go through a straight avenue of trees slightly uphill to a fork at the end (GPS 3). Go left and immediately pass the ruin 'Coral del Molinero' (GPS 4). Descend for 2km then follow the track across grassland to the Ermita de Buey (GPS 5) (3.42km from the Coral del Molinero). 1.24km after the Ermita turn left at a T-junction with a major dirt road (GPS 6). Stay on it for about 2.5 km to a major road. Go left follow the main road back to Frías.

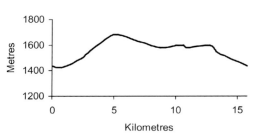

Ride 2: Moscardón

↔ 18km

⧗ ½ day

🍴 ▮

⛽ ▮

▣ 🙂

GPS points

N	W
1. *N40 19 881*	*W001 32 256*
2. *N40 16 529*	*W001 33 185*
3. *N40 16 661*	*W001 33 306*
4. *N40 18 510*	*W001 33 947*
5. *N40 18 435*	*W001 34 096*
6. *N40 19 233*	*W001 34 461*

Enter Moscardón on the main road coming from the A 1703 main road between Royuela and Terriente. As you enter the village take the vehicle track on the left signed to 'El Masegar' / 'Sendero de Los Atajos' (GPS 1). Follow this track for 6.5km until you pass a ruin on the left. 340m beyond this turn right off the main track (GPS 2). After 330m turn right again (GPS 3). Follow the most obvious track (ignoring minor turn-offs) for 700m until you pass a ruin on the right. 800m beyond is a 3-way junction where you bear to the right so that you pass in front of the tall, clearly visible yellow lookout tower. Continue to a house a few hundred metres beyond this tower and follow the track into woods to the left of this building. 2km from the house a track joins the one you are on from the right (GPS 4). Bear left. 300m further, another vehicle track cuts across you (GPS 5). Turn right. 1.5km further is a major crossroads with the main road from Frías to Moscardón (GPS 6). Turn right on the main road back to Moscardón.

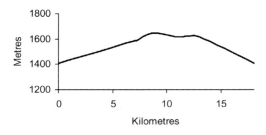

THIS IS A PLACE WHERE YOU NEED
TO TAKE A RIFLE NOT A CREDIT
CARD WHEN YOU GO TO PICK
SOMETHING UP FOR DINNER

Ride 3: Ermita de Buey

 34km

 1 day

 ■

■ ■

■ ☹

GPS points

N	W
1. N40 19 871	W001 32 711
2. N40 20 590	W001 32 766
3. N40 21 088	W001 34 165
4. N40 20 203	W001 34 437
5. N40 20 647	W001 35 464
6. N40 20 105	W001 37 221
7. N40 18 256	W001 37 063
8. N40 18 188	W001 37 037
9. N40 18 130	W001 35 435
10. N40 18 179	W001 34 729
11. N40 17 476	W001 35 199

Head out of Moscardón on the main road to Frías de Albarracín. About 1km from town turn right onto a track signed 'Balsa de Molino' (GPS 1). After 1.5km on the track turn left at a fork (GPS 2). 2.6km further the track swings steeply to the right and climbs for 650m. At the top, cross a field to farm buildings 500m away (GPS 3) where a major vehicle track crosses in front of the farm buildings. Turn left and descend for 800m then climb for 1km until a minor track appears on the right (initially going back downhill into the woods) (GPS 4). Follow this for a few kilometres until there is a short uphill section passing under power cables (GPS 5). Follow the rough direction of the pylons until you join a main road. Turn left and follow it to Frías de Albarracín. Go through this town and leave on the road heading to Tragacete and Cuenca. Just after leaving town you pass the ruins of a chapel. 300m further turn left onto a sandy vehicle track (GPS 6). Follow this for 3.3km until it climbs steeply through some switchbacks. At the summit follow the main track through a straight avenue of trees slightly uphill. At the end is a fork (GPS 7). Turn left. Pass the Del Molinero ruin (GPS 8). Descend for 2km through woods. At the bottom of the descent follow the track for 1.5km through meadows to the Ermita de Buey (GPS 9). 1.24km beyond the Ermita turn left at the T-junction with a major dirt road (GPS 10). Follow this for 2.5km and turn right onto another major track. After 1.62km along this track, turn left. (GPS 11). After 1.21km go left at a fork. After 1km further is a junction - go right. Other tracks join you. Follow the main track passing near a yellow fire tower. Continue 900m south of the tower to a ruin. 1.74km from the tower is a fork where you go left. 2.28km from the tower you meet a major vehicle track. Go left. Descend for 6.8km back to Moscardón.

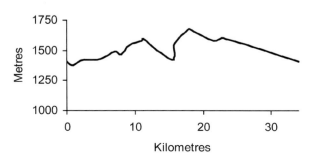

ALBARRACÍN RIDES

Ride 4: Las Pinturas Rupestres

⟷ **16.5km**

⧖ **½ day**

GPS points

N	W
1. N40 23 453	W001 25 077
2. N40 22 905	W001 25 349
3. N40 21 281	W001 24 079
4. N40 22 746	W001 24 106
5. N40 23 484	W001 24 310
6. N40 24 540	W001 25 964

From Albarracín take the road south-east towards the famous caves (with prehistoric paintings). On the edge of Albarracín go right at a fork and ignore the left going to the campsite. Continue for 2.4km from this junction then turn right onto a vehicle track (GPS 1) that immediately splits in two. Go right uphill for 1.35km until the track flattens and there is a junction (GPS 2). Go left and follow the track (Camino de Valdecuenca) for 3.5km. Turn left at the next junction (GPS 3). Descend for 1.8km to the GR 10. Turn left following red and white marker for 2.7km until the GR route meets the main road (GPS 4). Turn left onto the main road for 1.2km to a picnic site and information centre for the caves (Cuevas) on the right. Take the first right after the information centre. Follow this for 500m. There is a short ascent, a flat section then brief downhill. At the bottom of this descent the track curves to the right. Turn left on the bend onto a small GR 10 route down the Cabrerizo Gorge (GPS 5) (carrying your bike initially). Follow the trail through the gorge for 3.5km back to Albarracín (GPS 6).

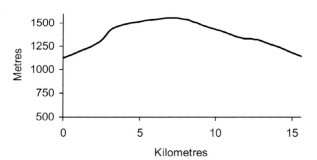

ACCOMMODATION

Los Palacios, Calle Los Palacios, 21, Albarracín, 978 700 327.
La Casa del Abuelo, Llano del Arrabal, no 22, 44100, Albarracín, 978 700 370.
Camping Cuidad de Albarracín.
Casa Rural and Casa Albergue, Rubiales, 978 681 043.
Casa de Santiago, 978 700 316.
Casa del Abuelo, 978 710 197, www.lacasadelbuelo.net.

IF ALBARRACÍN FEELS REMOTE,
TRAVELLING TO MOSCARDÓN,
FRÍAS DE ALBARRACÍN AND BEZAS
WILL KNOCK YOUR SOCKS OFF

 17km

 ½ day

 ▮

▮ ▮

▣ ☺

GPS points

	N	W
1.	N40 24 389	W001 21 537
2.	N40 22 411	W001 23 198
3.	N40 21 398	W001 22 266
4.	N40 22 894	W001 22 331
5.	N40 23 772	W001 21 709
6.	N40 24 389	W001 21 537

Ride 5: Gea de Albarracín

From Gea de Albarracín head out of town on the A1512 to Albarracín. Just before the km16 road marker turn left onto a vehicle track that soon goes over a bridge across the river. After about 400m go right at a fork (GPS 1) and follow the more substantial of two tracks. Climb for 7km to a main road (GPS 2). Turn left and follow the road to a major lay-by on your left after about 3km (GPS 3). A vehicle track descends away from the road. After only 100 metres ignore the left turn. 2.8km from the road you pass a spring and building (GPS 4) Descend for 4.45km from the road to a junction and stay on the main track ignoring the right turn. 250m further ignore the left turn (GPS 5). Rendezvous with the sandy track at (GPS 6). Turn right back to town.

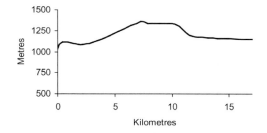

OTHER AREAS TO EXPLORE

There is a Via Verde route known as the 'Vía Verde de Ojos Negros' from Cella, north east of Albarracín through Teruel to Barracas 74kms away. It passes between the Sierra de Gúdar and Sierra del Javalambre. As it follows a disused railway line you will not be taxed technically but it cuts through some wild and stunning scenery.
Maps: Mapa del Instituto Geográfico Nacional,1:50.000 (no.s 566,567,587,590,613 and 614).

Cuenca is geographically nearby and offers similar biking but with more hardcore gradients. The meandering roads between the two locations makes progress slow going.

SIERRA DE MARINA ALTA

SIERRA DE MARINA ALTA
VALENCIA -
COMUNIDAD VALENCIANA

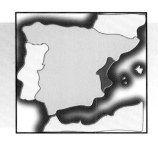

COMUNIDAD VALENCIANA

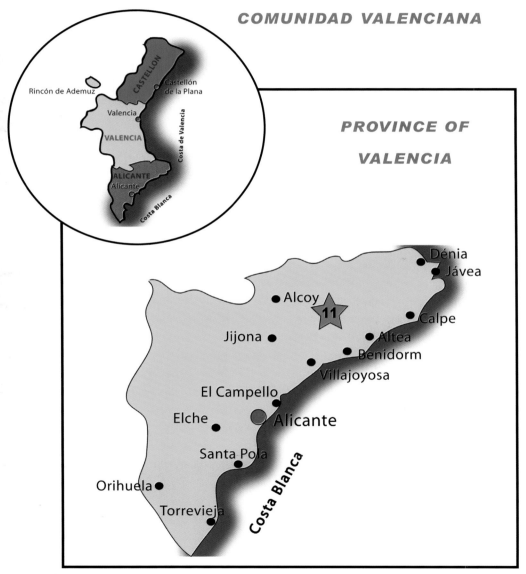

PROVINCE OF
VALENCIA

SIERRA DE MARINA ALTA
EASTERN SPAIN

Location

Rarely do you find a village geographically so close to a major city yet so utterly unaffected by its influence. As the crow flies, Castell de Castells is about 25km from Benidorm but the insanely steep, narrow and meandering mountain roads make the journey a long one even at the break-neck, joy-rider speeds adopted by the locals. This preservation from the coastal sprawl of the Costa Brava means Castell de Castells is a wonderful village where the old ways of life still linger. The only draw back is that there aren't very good local amenities to satisfy the appetites of go getting, nightlife loving riders. Be prepared with money, fuel, food and a pack of cards otherwise you may find yourself needing to spend time travelling back down to the metropolis for essential supplies and for something to do.

There is a superb free camping area just outside the village called El Castellet. Call the local lady who supervises it to unlock the bathrooms. They are very tidy. Most of the rides start and end at the campsite.

General Background

Today, Castell de Castells is a quaint rural retreat but the abundance of cave dwellings and rock paintings is indicative of the human presence that has been here for aeons. One of the best places to see these ancient dwellings is at the nearby village of La Vall d'Ebo. More recently the Moors inhabited the region and they built the highest castle in Andalucia on the Pena Del Castellet peak at 1050 metres. This monument gives its name to the village which, literally translated, means 'Castle of Castles'. Trails pass beneath these old ruins and it is worth clambering up to the castle to take in the views. This vantage point gives an excellent perspective of the town and locality. Below you are the vivid turquoise waters of the Guadalest reservoir some 700 metres straight down.

The Weather

Classic Mediterranean weather is experienced in the area so it is warm and sunny with comparatively mild winter weather and scorching summers. However, because the hills rise steeply up from sea level local microclimates are created. Snow is not uncommon in deep winter and there are some interesting evening mists that roll down from the hillsides when the sun goes down. The predominantly dry conditions and lack of rainfall means there is a great deal of rock and dust and very little vegetation. Trees are most notably absent making riding conditions harsh because there is no respite from the beating sun.

Protected Status

There is no protection of note to the local countryside making riding permissible practically anywhere.

Local Dangers

Ride well within your limits because good medical facilities are not close at hand. Ride in the morning and evening to escape the heat and take plenty of water.

Mountain Range
La Marina Alta.

Highest Peak
Pena La Yedra 1379m.

Getting There
✈ Alicante (70km).
🚌 Benidorm (30km).

Nearest Town/City
Castell de Castell/Benidorm (30km).

Equipment Type
XC

Recommended Bases
Castell de Castell, Campsite El Castellet.

Tourist Information
Castell de Castell Tourist Office, 965 518 067.

Ride Guides
Camilla & Martin Darburn, Mountain Activ, Calle San Vicente 18, 03793 Castell de Castells, 965 518 254, castells@darburn.com.

Body Repair
Casa Del Medico, 965 518 076.
Red Cross, 965 254 141.

THE AREA HAS A HISTORY OF
HUMANITY LIVING IN HILLTOP
HANGOUTS, LIKE THE CASTLE OF
CASTLES /CASTELL DE CASTELLS

☑ Equipment

Make sure you are able to carry plenty of water and you have
quick-drying cool clothing. Make sure you have with you all the
obvious spares that you are likely to need so that you do not
have to take a lengthy trip down to the coast for something as
simple as an inner tube. There are good bike shops in Benidorm
but it can take a day to go there and back. There is no need for
big tyres and it is nice to have thin, fast tyres that allow you to
climb quickly, however, you need something knobbly and strong
to cope with the abundance of rocky debris. A dry lube is
important due to the especially dusty tracks.

FR XC Freeride and Cross-Country

Cross-country bikes are most at home. The long vehicle track uphills
are always steep and long. You need stamina and a light bike to get
up as effortlessly as possible in the strong heat. The singletrack usually has sharp turns, sharp rocks, loose surfaces and
tricky drop-offs. Freeride bikes will love some of the descents so long as you have the strength to get them up hill.

DH Downhill

The descent from the highest castle to the free campsite is a superb descent but, on the
whole, heavy downhill rigs are not suited to these conditions.

👁 Local Observations

When you are exploring it is worth noting that some routes can look like major tracks that
must inevitably go somewhere interesting. However, they can end abruptly after a few
kilometres at a farmer's orchard or field. Quite often you can find yourself at a dead end
after a long time in the saddle with the only way back being the way you came. Well-
established routes are found traversing the hillsides. On the whole, much of the riding
consists of wide, dusty vehicle tracks. These routes are fairly easy to follow. Uphills are
usually tough. Singletrack is always steep, rocky, technical and hard to find.
Consequently paying the local guides for their services can pay dividends.

Maps 😐
Series:Mapa Topográfico Nacional de España, 1:25,000,
821-IV Castell de Castells.Buy in Benidorm.

Banks 😞

Fuel 😞

Bike Repair 😊 😐 😞
BeniBike Bicicletas, Calle Ruzafa, 16 local 14, Benidorm,
965 867 033.
Bicicletas Ricardo, AV Juan Carlos 1, 59, 965 459 914.
Bicimania Los Angeles, Av. Novelda, 131, 965 175 924.

Bike Hire 😞
Camilla & Martin Darburn, Mountain Activ, as before.

Other Activities
Golf, climbing, horse riding, paragliding, canyoning.

Day Off
There are prehistoric rock paintings and caves in and
around La Val d'Ebo. Experience the nightlife and resort
facilities of Benidorm. Enjoy the Costa Blanca (Altea is
worth a look).

Best Riding Times

J F M A M J J A S O N D

CASTELL DE CASTELLS RIDES

Ride 1: GR Route Around Town

↔ **6km**

⧖ **¼ day**

Ψ ■

⬦ ▰

⌗ ☺

GPS points

N	W
1. N38 43 289	W000 11 776
2. N38 43 042	W000 10 250
3. N38 43 067	W000 10 336

Start at the southern edge of Castell de Castells where the CV 752 main road skirts the bottom end of the town and there is a small bridge (GPS 1). Follow the main road south east towards Tarbena. Climb steeply for 4.2km until the main road stops ascending and a left turn appears on a right hand bend in the road. Turn onto this vehicle track (GPS 2). Follow it past two small houses. 60m from the road turn left at a fork. 60m further is a small dip in the track. Just as you start to rise out of this dip turn right down an obscure looking footpath (GPS 3). Follow the singletrack marked by GR red and white stripes. After 160m you reach a vehicle track. Turn left then immediately right as indicated by the paint markers. Continue on singletrack until the trail meets another vehicle track. Go right continuing downhill. After about 200m is another fork; go right. At the next junction go right. 180m from here you rejoin the main road. Go straight over the road and continue on the trail on the other side. Keep going downhill, passing the town tip. Follow the track back to the road and turn left to return to town.

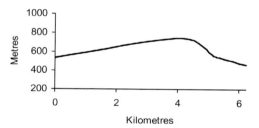

Ride 2: Lloma de l'Espinar peak

↔ **17km**

⧖ **¾ day**

Ψ ■

⬦ ▰

⌗ ☹

GPS points

N	W
1. N38 43 289	W000 11 776
2. N38 42 931	W000 09 649
3. N38 41 983	W000 10 619

Start at the southern edge of Castell de Castells where the CV 752 main road skirts the bottom end of town and there is a small bridge (GPS 1). Climb on the CV 752 towards Tarbena. After an arduous 4km uphill, the road levels out and becomes straight. Continue for 1.5km on fairly flat road until you pass a concrete marker saying '7km CV 752' on the left of the road. Take the next right after this point where there is a signboard saying 'Repoblacion Forestal' (GPS 2). Stay on the main gravel track ignoring any grassy turnings. Pass a sign saying 'Generalitat Valenciana'. Ignore the left and right turns just after. Follow the track as it climbs up to the Lloma de l'Espinar peak. After a total of 10.5km you reach the summit of the mountain where there is a major junction (GPS 3). Turn right. Descend on the major vehicle track following yellow and white markers and a low wall. At the next major cross roads near the ancient Moorish castle turn right and follow the track downhill back to the main road. Turn right to return to town.

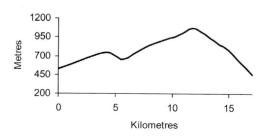

Ride 3: El Far and the PR168 to Castell

↔ **13km**

⧗ **½ day**

GPS points

N	W
1. N38 43 615	W000 11 772
2. N38 44 766	W000 11 734
3. N38 44 303	W000 11 936

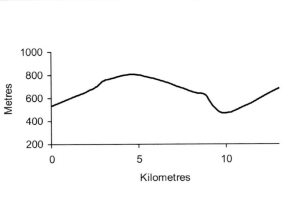

Head out of Castell on the CV 720 towards Benichembla. A few hundred metres outside town take the first major left that you come to (GPS 1). After a short distance there is a junction at some animal sheds. Turn right. 1km along this rough tarmac track is a fork. Go right. Ascend for 2.3km to an old farm building where the track becomes loose rubble making it nearly impossible to climb. At the first sign-posted junction turn right following the sign to 'El Far'. 2km further is another junction where there is a concrete bunker type construction. Turn right. Immediately after is another fork. Go right again. After 600m is a turning on your left going through some almond orchards follow this for 600m to a small tarmac road. Turn right downhill for 600m around a handful of hairpin bends keeping an eye out for a wooden sign post on your right signed PR 168 to Castell. This becomes singletrack at (GPS 2). Follow the singletrack until it drops you down into a riverbed. Follow the PR markers across the river and up the other bank onto the main road. The singletrack comes out on the main CV720 road (GPS 3). Turn right on the road to go back to Castell.

CASTELL DE CASTELLS **RIDES**

Ride 4: The PR 149 Castellet Circuit

↔ **10km**

⧗ **½ day**

GPS points

N	W
*1. **N38 43 289***	*W000 11 776*
*2. **N38 43 466***	*W000 12 613*
*3. **N38 42 570***	*W000 11 820*

From Castell de Castells (GPS 1) follow the CV 752 towards Facheca. After about 3.2km the road ceases to ascend and Castell de Castells starts to become obscured behind you. The road enters an avenue of pine trees and there is a road marker saying CV 720 (km 20). At this point there is a vehicle track going steeply up on the left (GPS 2). Turn up this vehicle track. Follow it for 1.8km to a sign posted junction. Ignore the steeper uphill and take the flatter left turn signed for 'Castellet PRV 149'. Follow the track for about 1.5km at the first sharp bend in the track a singletrack begins on the left and is signed to 'Area 20 Castellet' (GPS 3). Descend on this trail down to the free camping area. The town is easily found from the campsite.

ACCOMMODATION

Pensión Castells, Calle San Vicente 18, 03793 Castell de Castells, Alicante, Spain, 965 518 254 castells@darburn.com (English speaking).

Aparthotel Serrella, Calle Alcoy, 2, 03793 Castell de Castells, 965 518 138.

Casa Pilar, 965 518 157

Campsite El Castellet, Castell de Castells.

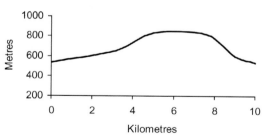

OTHER AREAS TO EXPLORE

Alicante is home to a large purpose built dirt jump and BMX type circuit. It is the national circuit and found at San Vicente de Raspeig. From Castell it is possible to ride downhill to the coast. It is worth arranging this with the local guides. Just south east of Castell de Castells, off the CV 752 is a large airstrip. The views from there are impressive but can also give you a good perspective of where to look for potential trails.

SIERRA DE ESPUÑA

SIERRA DE ESPUÑA
REGIÓN DE MURCIA

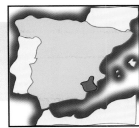

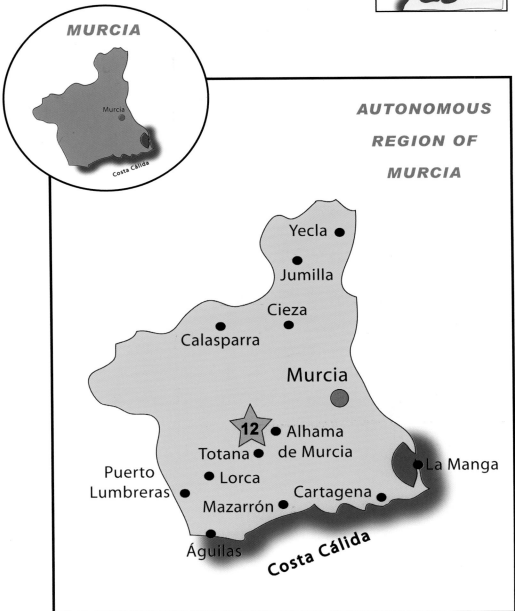

MURCIA

Murcia

Costa Cálida

AUTONOMOUS

REGION OF

MURCIA

Yecla ●

● Jumilla

Cieza ●

Calasparra ●

Murcia

12 ● Alhama
Totana ● de Murcia

La Manga ●

Puerto
Lumbreras ● Lorca ●

Cartagena ●
Mazarrón ●

Águilas ● Costa Cálida

SIERRA DE ESPUÑA
SOUTH EAST SPAIN

Location

The Sierra Espuña are found in the little known province of Murcia. The bulk of the riding is found around the village of El Berro. This small settlement is only a few kilometres from the towns of Alhama de Murcia and Totana but long winding roads make it feel very isolated. The larger towns are themselves the quiet backwaters of Spain but with just over 100 inhabitants, it seems El Berro has been forgotten even by the Spaniards.

General Background

There are deep valleys that have been cut by powerful streams that have charged downhill from the melting snow for millennia. The power of these watercourses is derived from the impressive range of altitude found in these hills; they rise from 200m up to 1500m in a fairly confined space. The area was reforested at the beginning of the 20th century and is still heralded as a model of hydrological and forestry reclamation. It was declared a Natural Park in 1978 and in 1995 the badlands of the Barrancos de Gebas were added. The most important local features are the Pozos de Nieves or ice houses. In the 15th and 16th centuries snow was compacted into ice high up in the mountains and brought down by mule. To carry this traffic some of the most staggering singletrack in Spain was created. The man-made paths are narrow with plenty of switchbacks giving the feel of purpose built mountain biking trails.

The Weather

The climate in the region surrounding the Espuña Natural Park is fairly tame Mediterranean weather. However, inside the park (where the riding takes place) there are microclimates created by the sudden change in altitude from the flat plains to high peaks. The average annual temperature in the mountains is 13.8°C, 4.5°C lower than the average for the region. The rainfall can be torrential and falls mainly in spring and autumn. Winter is very cold when there is a lot of snow.

Protected Status

Despite its ecological importance, the local authorities tolerate off-road riding practically anywhere.

Local Dangers

The altitude and dry air can have a noticeable affect on visitors who exert themselves so start your riding gently and acclimatise. Forest fires are an extreme hazard in the summer. Be mindful of the isolation and make sure someone knows where you are as bad weather moves in quickly especially in early spring and late autumn.

Equipment

Disc brakes and good tyres are important for braking on the long, rocky descents. Shin protectors and lightweight long sleeved tops are wise protection against the whipping undergrowth. Light bikes with bounce are useful as they make the uphills tolerable but a robust and active free-ride bike will really get a work out on some of the long, technical descents.

Mountain Range
Sierra Espuña, Cordillera Bética..

Highest Peak
Espuña 1583m.

Getting There
✈ Alicante (120km), Almeria (200km), Málaga (380km)
🚂 Murcia (30km).

Nearest Town/*City*
Alhama de Murcia /*Murcia (30km).*

Equipment Type
XC FR

Recommended Bases
El Berro, Alhama de Murcia, Totana.

Tourist Information
Oficina Municipal de Turismo, Plaza de La Constitucion, Alhama de Murcia, 968 633 512.

Ride Guides
Ask at the Camping Sierra Espuña, El Berro.

Body Repair
Accident and Emergency, Alhama de Murcia, 968 630 369.
Red Cross, Alhama de Murcia, C/ Capitán Portola, 968 630 930.

INTENSE FRAGRANCES
PERMEATE THE AIR IN THE
WARMER MONTHS. RIDING
HAS NEVER SMELT SO GOOD

PROS + CONS
+ Breathtaking hand-built singletrack
+ Extreme natural beauty
+ Tranquil, peaceful and isolated
- A poor area with little infrastructure
- High frequency of torrential storms

XC Cross-Country

An excellent cross-country retreat. The high altitude, long steep climbs and technical descents make the area full of variety for riders with light, slightly bouncy bikes.

There are very long climbs that are rewarded with equally long descents and a couple of roadside restaurants nestling in the mountains make it a fantastic holiday experience.

FR Freeride

The icehouse trails that cling to the steep sides of the valleys really sum up what free ride mountain biking is all about. The challenging descents can continue for close to an hour. In places the trails are so

treacherously thin and the undergrowth so intrusive that you need to be cautious. Disc brakes are advisable.

DH Downhill

Unless you have vehicle support to meet you at the bottom, downhill rigs are just too heavy to use in this area.

👁 Local Observations

The balmy heat produces an intense sappy fragrance of pine and rosemary which permeates the air in the warmer months. These aromatic trails are not for the feint of heart or those with a fear of falling. Many routes cling precariously to the edges of steep valleys with long drops if you miss your turn. The Spanish tend to stick to the well-trodden central paths and, after five minutes riding from some of these busy spots, you quickly find yourself away from the melee. It is reassuring to know that you can encounter these occasional oases of civilisation so that you can revitalise.

Check the El Mirador bar/restaurant near Gebas where local bikers hang out at weekends. At the weekends (even in the winter months) the cafes and walks are filled with locals. Fortunately these are big hills that easily absorb the crowds.

Maps 🙁
Series: Mapa Topográfico Nacional de España: 1. Alcantarilla 933, III Alhama de Murcia and 2. Coy 932, IV, 1:25,000. Buy in Murcia.

Banks 😐
Alhama de Murcia & Totana.

Fuel 😐
Alhama de Murcia & Totana.

Bike Hire 🙁

Other Activities
Hiking, climbing, paragliding and botany.

Day Off
The ice houses/Pozos de Los Nieves are an interesting diversion. Head to the Costa Cálida for unspoilt beaches and the Mar Menor/ La Manga for seaside restaurants. Wander around the compact city of Murcia.

Best Riding Times

J F M A M J J A S O N D

SIERRA DE ESPUÑA RIDES

Ride 1: The Barranco de Leiva Valley

↔ **24km**

⧖ **¾ day**

GPS points

N	W
1. N37 52 023	*W001 30 236*
2. N37 51 906	*W001 29 884*

Turn right out of the El Berro campsite and head south/south-west away from town for 2.3km on the main road until you climb up to a T-junction. Turn right and follow the road until it starts to descend down into the Barranco de Leiva valley. At the bottom you pass the Casa Leiva recreation area with barbecue facilities. 200m after the road crosses the Leiva stream, turn left onto a gated vehicle track signed 'Camino Forestal Fuente Bermeja' (GPS 1). Descend on this track ignoring the first left after 100m. 350m further follow the track to the left (ignoring the right going to the Fuente Bermeja spring). 880m from the road a singletrack starts on the left (GPS 2). (Ignore the path 180m before this). The singletrack you want is identifiable because it has a manmade irrigation ditch (a leat) running alongside it. If you reach the Refugio Bermeja you have gone too far. Once found follow the singletrack as it runs parallel but above the track heading towards the Refugio Bermeja. After a few kilometres you

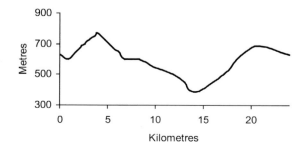

reach a vehicle track. Turn left on this, go around the first bend then continue on singletrack that resumes by some large boulders. Aim for the large pipe that can be seen going over a ridge up ahead. The trail eventually reaches the foot of this pipe. Climb over it and continue on the trail on the other side. It soon drops down onto a vehicle track. Turn left and you come out by a group of houses at a small place called Carmona. Follow the vehicle track away from these farm buildings past citrus groves and on to the C3315 main road that runs between Gebas and Alhama de Murcia. Turn left and follow the road back to El Berro.

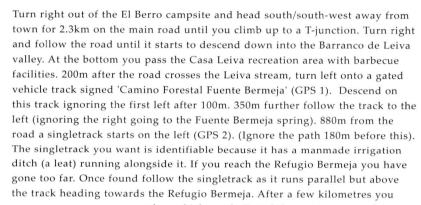

THESE AROMATIC TRAILS ARE NOT
FOR THE FAINT OF HEART OR THOSE
WITH A FEAR OF FALLING. YOU CAN
RUN OUTTA SPACE REAL FAST

Ride 2: To the Pico de la Garita

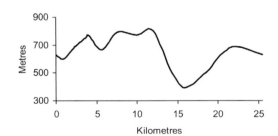

25km

¾ day

GPS points

N	W
1. N37 51 207	W001 30 355
2. N37 52 574	W001 28 051

From the Fuente Bermeja track mentioned in ride 1 continue heading south-west on the main road so that you climb out the other side of the Leiva valley. Follow the road that goes past the Centro de Interpretación, a large building on your right. Continue past this for about 1.5km until you reach a lay-by where there is a vehicle track signed 'Camino Forestal Garita Del Turullon' (GPS 1). Turn onto this track. After 450m there is a fork where you turn right. Follow the track uphill for 2km to the radio mast and fire look at the top of the Pico de la Garita mountain. Although the track seems to end, imagine a line going straight through the hut and carrying on the other side. Follow this approximate direction and there is a very tiny path going down the left-hand side of the huge, steep firebreak. At the bottom of this tough descent, the fire break goes into a dip before climbing uphill again, turn right onto the singletrack on the far right-hand side of this dip. Descend on this singletrack for about 1.5km until you reach a vehicle track that switchbacks tightly. Go just 20m downhill on this track and turn left off it onto more singletrack, which resumes before you have even gone around the first bend in the main track. Continue until you reach a fork in the path where you go right downhill (GPS 2). At the next junction turn left and then first right after 15 metres. Here the trail becomes a vehicle track. Follow it to a group of farm buildings at Carmona. Follow the vehicle track away from these buildings past citrus groves and on to the C3315 main road between Gebas and Alhama de Murcia. Turn left and follow the road back to El Berro.

SIERRA DE ESPUÑA RIDES

Ride 3: Refugio La Bermeja

↔ **18km**

⧗ **¾ day**

🍴 ▨

🛢 ■

🔲 ☹

GPS points

N	W
1. N37 51 207	W001 30 355
2. N37 52 574	W001 28 051
3. N37 51 973	W001 28 590

Follow ride 2 so that you climb the 'Camino Forestal Garita Del Turullon' (GPS 1) up to the radio mast and fire look at the top of the Pico de la Garita. Again follow the trail down the firebreak and pick up the singletrack. Continue on this superb path until you reach the fork (GPS 2). This time turn left. Follow the singletrack slightly uphill for 1.5 km until you cross a small irrigation canal/leat. Soon after you reach a confused junction where lots of little paths criss-cross one another, there is also a large vehicle track to your left. Take the singletrack on the far right (GPS 3). The trail follows the small leat. Continue on the most obvious trail ignoring minor trails. Carefully descend a very steep section and continue undulating until the trail ends at a steep descent and comes out behind the Refugio La Bermeja. Turn left onto the vehicle track in front of this building. Follow it for about 1.2km to the main road. Turn right to return to El Berro.

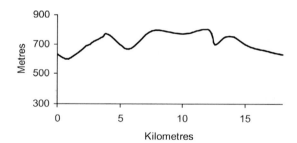

THE HIGH ALTITUDE, LONG
STEEP CLIMBS AND TECHNICAL
DESCENTS MAKE THE AREA
FULL OF VARIETY FOR RIDERS

Ride 4: El Berro to Carmona

19km

½ day

From the El Berro Campsite entrance turn right and follow the road for about 20m to a 90° left hand bend in the road where two tracks start on the right. Take the left hand path and climb steeply on this track until it levels out then ends at a T-junction with the a tarmac road. Turn right and after a few hundred metres turn left down an obvious track with a chain across it. Descend through a couple of switchbacks turning right at the first junction. It is easy to miss but appears just as the track levels out and starts to go slightly uphill. The track becomes progressively difficult to follow and eventually ends at a clearing where there is a firebreak in front of you rising up to a small summit. There are three small trails visible. Take the path down hill on the left into the trees. Although initially vague, this singletrack quickly develops. At the first T-junction turn left onto a major track that is rutted by the passage of streams. At the first major bend rejoin the singletrack that is slightly obscured from view by a large boulder. Head for the large, silver pipe that can be seen going over a ridge up ahead. The trail eventually leads you to the foot of this pipe where you cross the small concrete bridge and continue the trail on the other side. It continues for a short section before dropping down onto a dust road. Turn left onto the dust track and follow it past the farm buildings at Carmona until it brings you out on to the C3315 road. Turn left and follow the road back to El Berro.

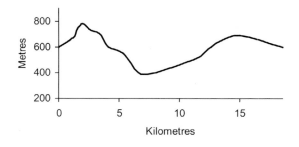

SIERRA DE ESPUÑA RIDES

Ride 5: Umbria de Peña Apartada

25km

¾ day

Y ■

◆ ■

▣ ☺

GPS points

N   *W*

1. *N37 51 307   W001 34 087*

Follow the main road from El Berro towards the summit of Espuña. There is a military radar that look like a giant golf ball on top of the mountain. As you climb up to these structures you come to a road junction near the summit opposite which there is a vehicle track called the 'Umbria de Peña Apartada' (GPS 1). Join this vehicle track. It is a straightforward to follow ride and ends at the main road, which you can follow back to El Berro.

ACCOMMODATION

El Berro

Camping Sierra Espuña, El Berro, 968 668 038, www.campingelberro.com / www.ctv.es/USERS/sierra_espuna. Log cabins available.

Alhama de Murcia

Hostal Pagán, Autovia Del Mediterráneo, (Salida Sur Librilla), 968 658 166.
Hotel Los Bartolos, C. Alfonso X, 1, Alhama de Murcia, 968 632 661.

Gebas

Cortijo Las Golondrinas, Ecoespuña, C/1° de Mayo, Gebas, 968 636 205.

Totana

La Santa, Santuario de Sta Eulalia, s/n, Totana, 968 427 545, turismolasanta@ayto-totana.net www.ayto-totana.net/lasanta.

OTHER AREAS TO EXPLORE

Don't bother looking-you will not find any trails better than here!

If you want an easy day explore the Vía Verdes in this area. The Vía Verde del Campo de Cartagena is a 51km route from Totana, through the Sierra Espuna, to the coast (Cartagena). The Vía Verde del Noroeste is a 48km run from Baños de Mula to Caravaca de la Cruz, passing through the stunning 'badlands' of the area.

Southern Spain

CAZORLA NATURAL PARK

SIERRAS DE CAZORLA AND SEGURA
JAÉN - ANDALUCÍA

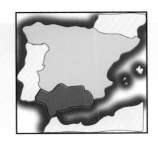

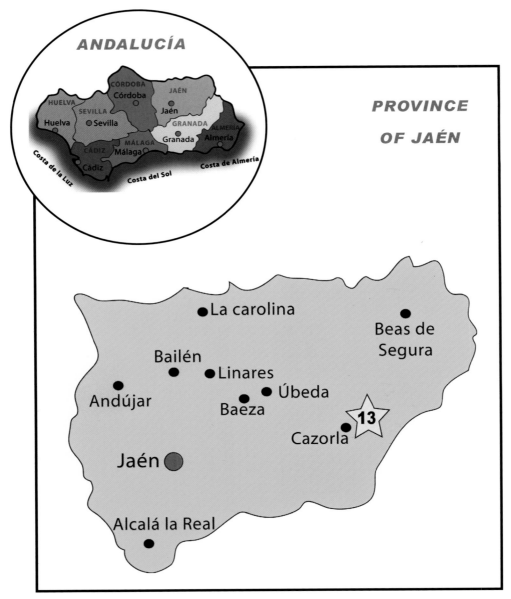

ANDALUCÍA

HUELVA
CÓRDOBA
Córdoba
SEVILLA
Huelva
Sevilla
JAÉN
Jaén
GRANADA
Granada
ALMERÍA
Almería
CÁDIZ
MÁLAGA
Málaga
Cádiz
Costa de la Luz
Costa del Sol
Costa de Almería

PROVINCE

OF JAÉN

La carolina

Beas de
Segura

Bailén

Linares

Andújar

Úbeda

Baeza

Cazorla

13

Jaén

Alcalá la Real

SIERRAS DE CAZORLA AND SEGURA
SOUTHERN SPAIN

Location

The best riding takes place in the Guadalquivir River Valley and on the slopes of the Sierra De Cazorla Mountains. These are located in the southwest of a massive Natural Park called the 'Cazorla, Segura and Las Villas Natural Park'. Cazorla is the focal point for the region and it sits on the edge of this protected region beneath the crag de Los Halcones.

General Background

The Natural Park is Spain's largest at 2143km² or 214,300 hectares and includes several mountain ranges. The parkland is prime hunting land and the local dishes of wild game are superb. Additionally the region is one of the largest olive oil producing regions in the world. Outside of the park 80% of the workable land is put to this use and Jaén province provides 10% of the world's olive oil. The exceptional quality of the oil means it is given a 'Denominación de Origen' the equivalent of the 'Appellation Controllée' given to French wines. There is a noticeable enthusiasm for mountain biking amongst the locals and it is possible to find groups who go riding at the weekends.

The Weather

The area experiences extreme weather conditions. It is cold in winter, January being extremely harsh with huge amounts of rain and snow. Spring and autumn are changeable, often with severe cloudbursts. Summers are hot and dry especially August which can be blistering. As you enter the park you can see the barriers that are used to close the roads when they become impassable due to storms or forest fires.

Protected Status

The area is a Natural Park but within the Guadalquivir River Valley there is a specially protected region that is marked on the local maps. Riding is only permitted on vehicle tracks within this zone, the only exception being the Rio Barosa ride.

Local Dangers

Forest fires are a serious threat in the summer when the scorched woodland and insane summer heat create a tinderbox and fire control is made difficult by the lack of access roads.

Mountain Range
Sierra de Cazorla, Sierras Subbéticas, Cordillera Bética.

Highest Peak
The Cabanas Peak 2026m.

Getting There
Málaga (310km), Madrid (435km), Alicante (510km).
Teruel (30km).

Nearest Town/City
Cazorla/*Ubeda (50km)*.

Equipment Type
XC

Recommended Bases
Cazorla, Arroyo Frio.

Tourist Information
Centro de Interpretación Torre del Vinagre, in the Guadalquivir valley. Oficina de Turismo Municipal, Paseo del Santo Cristo 17, 953 710 112.

Ride Guides
Excursiones Cazorla, 639 993 545, Quercus, 953 720 115, Bujarkay Borosa, 81 Coto Rios, 953 713 011.

Body Repair
Cazorla casualty 953 720 204, Quesada surgery, 953 734 205 Castril surgery 958 720 182.

LOCAL OLIVE OILS FROM THE
REGION ARE USED TO
PREPARE TASTY TAPAS TITBITS
FROM THE MOUNTAIN TOPS

PROS + CONS
+ Excellent singletrack
+ Extreme natural beauty
+ Interesting local food
- Remote
- Tough ascents
- Harsh weather

☑ Equipment

The singletrack is fast and flowing but there are regular rock gardens making a full suspension cross-country bike a good choice. Lightweight hard-tails are preferable for some of the serious uphills where walking is sometimes required but you need good skills to keep them under control on the technical descents.

XC Cross-Country

For incredibly tranquil long spins on forest roads and country lanes, there are enormous unexplored zones deep in the heart of the park. They are inaccessible to most because of the poor road network. Look around the towns of Siles, Hornos de Segura and Santiago de la Espada for virgin cross-country routes.

FR Freeride

The best singletrack and technical trails are found around Cazorla. They are kept open and well main-

tained by the regular tourist trade in the Cazorla region. Although the rest of the park looks promising on the map, low visitor numbers means that tenacious vegetation quickly swallows small, technical trails.

DH Downhill

Little of interest.

👁 Local Observations

Weather can close in rapidly and the best rides climb some serious peaks that are often far cooler than in the valleys. The singletracks around Cazorla are mainly ancient Moorish trade routes and are so well constructed that it is like riding down a garden path. This makes it easy to forget that you are a long way into the wilderness. Riding here is serious. Be well prepared and have a very clear idea of where you are going. If you do a little hard work you will find it is a sanctum of sensational singletrack!

Maps 🙂
Series: Editorial Alpina (green series), 1:40 000, Sierra de Cazorla. Buy in Cazorla.

Banks 🙂
Cazorla and Arroyo Frío.

Fuel 😐
Cazorla, Burunchel and there is one north of Arroyo Frío in the Guadalquivir valley.

Bike Repair 😞
Deportivo Mundo, 953 721 282.
Bicicletas Arriba, Úbeda, 953 750 893.

Bike Hire 😞

Other Activities
Fishing, canoeing, canyoning, rock-climbing, absailing, hiking, 4x4 trips, hunting.

Day Off
Visit the olive oil museum. Trout fishing. Eating - The Cueva de Juan Pedro in the Plaza de Santa María has particularly good meals.

Best Riding Times

J F M A M J J A S O N D

SIERRA DE CAZORLA RIDES

Ride 1: The Rio Borosa and the Cerrada de Elias

↔ 33km

⧗ 1 day

GPS points

N	W
1. N38 00 931	W002 51 735

From the 'Centro de Interpretacion Torre del Vinagre' in the Guadalquivir River valley (9km north of Arroyo Frio) follow the road for 1km to a fish farm (piscifactoria). Opposite is a car park where the Rio Borosa flows under the road (GPS 1). Take the vehicle track upstream on the left of the river. After 3.3km is a fork. Go right to the 'Cerrada de Elias', a wooden walkway through a narrow gorge. After 7.5km the vehicle track ends at the Central Electricia water pumping station. You can continue for 8km (walking and riding) up the very steep footpath that passes under spectacular waterfalls to the 'Collado de la Fuente Bermejo'. Retrace your steps to return. NB closed in winter.

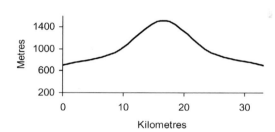

Ride 2: Casa Forestal De Prado Redondo

↔ 10km

⧗ ½ day

GPS points

N	W
1. N37 54 273	W002 57 719
2. N37 54 906	W002 58 874
3. N37 54 888	W002 58 922
4. N37 54 983	W002 59 727
5. N37 54 741	W002 59 692
6. N37 54 759	W002 59 747

Follow the main road up to the Hotel/Parador El Adelantado. At the hotel entrance turn right onto a vehicle track that (after 70m) goes past the Casa Refugio Sacejo (GPS 1). Follow signs for 'Comienzo Senda'. Ascend on a rough vehicle track through woods for 3km to a 3-way junction on the ridge of the mountain where high fences appear in front of you. Turn right and descend for 1.3km before entering a pinewood where the trail descends steeply and ends at the 'Casa Forestal De Prado Redondo' (GPS 2). Go to the left of the clearing that surrounds this building and pick up the GR marked path 50m from the forestry hut (GPS 3). After 500m the path meets a stream (often dry) near an electrical pylon. Follow the path along the stream. After a kilometre it descends to the 'Ermita de la Cabeza' (GPS 4). From the entrance to the church, descend for a few hundred metres on a vehicle track to the main road below. Cross the road to the viewpoint/ mirador (GPS 5) and descend on the singletrack to the right of it into Cazorla (GPS 6).

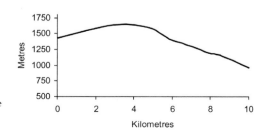

UPHILLS CAN BE INSANELY STEEP AND
APPEAR TO GO ON FOREVER.
NOWHERE IS IT MORE IMPORTANT TO
KEEP A POSITIVE FRAME OF MIND

Ride 3: The Parador 'El Adelantado' to Cazorla Town

7 km

½ day

GPS points

N	W
1. *N37 54 600*	*W002 56 514*
2. *N37 54 600*	*W002 56 514**
3. *N37 54 600*	*W002 56 514*

From the Hotel/Parador 'El Adelantado' descend for 3km down the main road to the spring and Casa Forestal - 'Fuente del Oso' (GPS 1). From here, follow the GR 7 footpath uphill signed "Cazorla 4hrs 10". Follow the red and white GR markers to Cazorla. Turn left at the fork 0.7km from the Fuente del Oso. The trail undulates through woods then climbs up and out of the valley. A long descent to La Iruela/Cazorla follows. After 3 km, a main road appears below and you reach a fork in the path (GPS 2*). Turn right downhill (ignore the red and white cross indicating the end of the GR route). 400m further is a junction. Go right downhill and you drop down onto the main road near Cazorla (GPS 3).

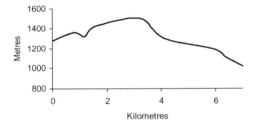

Extension

To make a gruelling circuit of ride 3, at (GPS 2*) continue on the GR 7 instead of descending to the road. Climb very steeply up a grassy slope, into some woods and on to the 'Casa Forestal de Prado Redondo' (GPS 4). Take the trail behind this building marked with red and white cross that indicates this is not the GR 7 (GPS 5). After a long

GPS points

N	W
2. *N37 54 600*	*W002 56 514**
* From ride 3 *	
4. *N37 54 921*	*W002 58 877*
5. *N37 54 906*	*W002 58 874*
6. *N37 54 273*	*W002 57 719*

ascent is a junction at a high fence. Turn left ignoring the trail that follows the tall fence to your right. The trail becomes a vehicle track and descends for about 3km returning to the hotel/ Parador (GPS 6). Go left on the main road to return to Fuente del Oso.

SIERRA DE CAZORLA RIDES

Ride 4: The Castillo de Cinco Esquines y de Salvatierra

↔ **11km**

⧗ **½ day**

Ψ ▨

🜄 ▨

▣ ☺

GPS points

N	W
1. *N37 55 263*	*W002 59 604*
2. *N37 55 759*	*W002 59 747*
3. *N37 53 505*	*W002 59 781*
4. *N37 53 616*	*W003 00 406*

From La Iruela take the road to El Chorro (GPS 1). After a short distance you pass a left turning going to the Ermita Virgen de la Cabeza (GPS 2). After about 3km the road is cut by a barrier (GPS 3). Continue for 2.2km from the barrier (6km from La Iruela) until you reach an information board on your right where a footpath begins on your right (GPS 4). As you head down this path the castle 'Castillo de Cinco Esquines y de Salvatierra' can be seen directly ahead. It soon veers to the left away from the castle. Follow it to the monastery 'Monasterio de Monte Sion' (an unremarkable group of buildings) where a confusion of tracks turns to the right. Turn right and go downhill on any of these tracks; they all return to Cazorla.

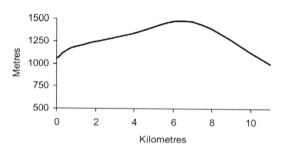

THE WORD ISOLATED BEGINS
TO TAKE ON NEW MEANING
WHEN YOU VENTURE INTO THE
VASTNESS OF THE PARK

SIERRA DE SEGURA **RIDES**

Ride 5: Puntal de la Ajedrea

40km

½ day

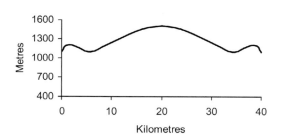

From the Camping Fuente de la Canalica head onto the main road and turn right up the hill. Take the first left after 1.5km. Descend for 4.3km until you cross the Baranco de los Tejos - a stream. Ascend on the vehicle track up to the Puntal de la Ajedrea peak 1507m where there is a forest fire look out point. Return the same way.

SIERRA DE SEGURA RIDES

↔ **30km**

⧖ **½ day**

🍴 ▮

💧 ▮

⬚ 😊

Ride 6: Around the Tranco Reservoir

Start in Hornos and head out of town on the main road towards Cortijos Nuevos. Take the first left after 4km at the junction that heads towards Canada Morales and Tranco. Turn off for the vehicle track around the lake's edge. Stay on the track for 7.3km then turn off for La Platera. Turn right onto a vehicle track opposite the small bar in town. Follow it until you descend back to the lake. Turn right on the track around the lake.

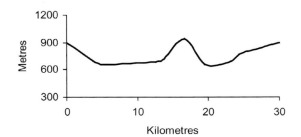

ACCOMMODATION

If you want to experience the wilderness at close quarters there are campsites and a range of accommodation in the Guadalquivir valley. There is also the relatively expensive Parador El Adelantado.

Cazorla
H*** Ciudad de Cazorla, 953 721 700.
HA*** Villa Turística, 953 710 100.
Hs Betis, 953 720 740.
Camping Cortijo San Isicio, 953 721 280 (should be open all year).

Arroyo Frío
H** Montana, 953 727 011
HA*** Los Enebros, 953 727 110.
Camping Los Enebros, 953 727 110.

H*** El Adelantado Parador Nacional, 953 727 075.

Hotel de Montana Riogazas, 953 124 035

WATERFALLS CASCADE FROM THE ROCKS AS BIRDS OF PREY SOAR MAJESTICALLY ABOVE, TROUT FEED IN THE CRYSTAL STREAMS WHERE WILD DEER DRINK THE COOL WATERS; A SCENE FROM BAMBI OR CAZORLA NATURAL PARK? YOU DECIDE.

OTHER AREAS TO EXPLORE

The area around Siles has a good potential for riding and there are a couple of worthwhile singletracks to find on the hills above that town. Look out for rides around: Valedeazores Lagoon, Nava del Espino near La Mesa, El Cantalar, Puerto de Tiscar by the Garbanzal ravine to the Zamora pass, Puerto de las Palomas to the Fuente de la Zarza and the Sauco stream.

The Vía Verde del Aceite is a 55km stretch of easy riding between Jaén and the river Guadajoz, passing through 2 tunnels and over 9 viaducts.

MASSIF DE CABO DE GATA

MASSIF DE CABO DE GATA
ALMERÍA - ANDALUCÍA

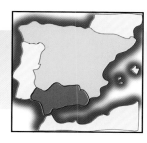

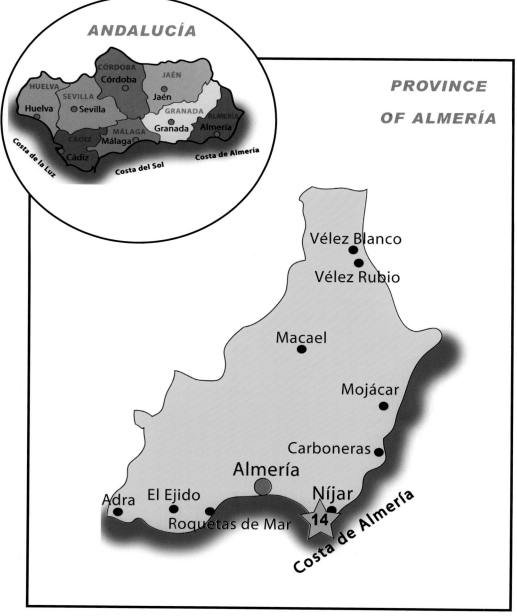

ANDALUCÍA

HUELVA
Huelva
SEVILLA
Sevilla
CÓRDOBA
Córdoba
JAÉN
Jaén
GRANADA
Granada
ALMERÍA
Almería
MÁLAGA
Málaga
CÁDIZ
Cádiz
Costa de la Luz
Costa del Sol
Costa de Almería

PROVINCE
OF ALMERÍA

Vélez Blanco
Vélez Rubio
Macael
Mojácar
Carboneras
Almería
Adra
El Ejido
Roquetas de Mar
Níjar
14
Costa de Almería

MASSIF CABO DE GATA

SOUTHERN SPAIN

Location

Cabo de Gata is found on the south-eastern tip of the Iberian Peninsular in the province of Almería on the Mediterranean coast. It is one of the most southerly points in Spain. The area is a Natural Park having been designated a land and marine reserve in 1987. The major city - Almería - is a thriving commercial hubbub.

General Background

Farming is the major industry and much of the land is sheathed in plastic under which crops are cultivated. The polythene wrapped countryside is ugly but emphasizes the beauty of the untouched Natural Park. The harsh, dry conditions have kept human activity to a minimum. The area has a history as a film set. The sand dunes were used in the film 'Lawrence of Arabia'. In the northwest of the park, wedged between the Sierra Alhamilla and the Sierras de Los Filabres, is the Paraje Natural Desierto de Tabernas where Serge Leone filmed Spaghetti Westerns. Cabo de Gata was a volcanically active area and rich mineral deposits meant mining for gold, galena and silver occurred during the 19th and 20th Centuries. Mining has stopped and whole villages have been abandoned leaving ghost towns such as Rodalquilar and Las Presillas Bajas.

The Weather

Due to the rain-shadow effect of the Sierra Nevada and the Sierra de Alhamilla, the area receives very little rainfall. All the moisture is sapped from the air by these land masses and the resultant dry air combined with over 3,000 hours of sunshine a year creates the driest region in Europe; indeed it is classified as a desert. It is not quite the hottest place in Spain but it is the driest.

Protected Status

Much of the Cabo de Gata Natural Park is made up of private land that has been voluntarily surrendered to the protection of the park. Other than staying off private land, there are few riding restrictions apart from the normal behaviour expected in Natural Parks (see introduction).

Local Dangers

The trail surfaces along the coast have light and loose volcanic rock and stones tend to ping up from under your tyres making 'rock shocks' commonplace. The combination of shifting surfaces and sheer drops make some of the cliff top trails precarious but exhilarating. There are no soft landings in this dry area and often nothing to prevent you toppling into the sea.

Mountain Range
Sierra de Cabo de Gata.

Highest Peak
493m.

Getting There
Almería (20km),
Malaga (200km), Alicante (290km).
Almería (20km).

Nearest Town/City
San José/Almería (20km).

Equipment Type

Recommended Bases
XC

San José, Los Escullos/La Isleta, Las Negras and Agua Amarga.

Tourist Information
Old Town, Calle Diputacion No 4., Albarracín.
Calle de Tomas Nogues 1, 978 602 279.
www.degata.com.

Ride Guides
Grupo J126, C/ Correo, San José, 950 380 299
grupoj126@larural.es.

Body Repair
Alcazaba ambulance service, 950 255 730.
Nijar Health Centre, 950 360 278.

A LAND OF OPPOSITES
WHERE STUNNING
JUXTAPOSITIONS CONSTANTLY
ASSAULT YOUR SENSES

PROS + CONS
+ Always dry and sunny
+ Good winter riding
+ Peaceful, quiet beaches
- Limited riding
- Isolated
- No killer descents

☑ Equipment

Dry chain lube is important. Lightweight hard-tails are at home because they require minimum effort to pedal in the extreme heat. Cool quick drying clothing and plenty of water carrying equipment essential.

XC Cross-Country

All the riding is suitable for those who like cross-country riding and don't mind road riding.

FR Freeride

Very little serious descending. Check out the mountains around Nijar for hard core trails.

DH Downhill

The extinct volcanoes between Rodalquillar and Los Albaricoques have some downhills if you can lug your rig to the top in the heat.

👁 Local Observations

Try to ride early in the day. Although midday can be hot, the real heat seems to come mid afternoon at about 4.00pm. Burning your calves, forearms, neck and even ears is easy on a long ride along the sea front. Put plenty of cream on. Carry plenty of water.

Cabo is an ideal place to meander along the coast stopping off for a cooling swim in some of the secluded beaches before visiting a small coastal fishing village to relax and refuel. Although there is not an abundance of single track and the highest peak in the park is only 493m, there are extremely good reasons to ride here. The trails are dry, rugged and fast, with stunning views of the sea. The uphills are never particularly long. It is rare to find such a stunning seaside location that hasn't been inundated with high rise coastal development. It is not an area that is rich in radical trails; rather, it is a romantic riding retreat.

📍 Maps 🙂
Series: Editorial Alpina - Cabo de Gata Níjar Parque Natural 1:50,000. Buy in San Jose.

💰 Banks 🙂
Cabo de Gata, San José.

💧 Fuel 😐
Km 6.5 between San José and Cabo de Gata village.

🔧 Bike Repair 😐
Good shops near the Carrefour supermarket in Almería.

🚲 Bike Hire
Deportes Media Luna, San José, 950 380 462.
Most shops in Almería.

📷 Other Activities
Quad biking, horse riding, scuba diving, windsurfing, boat trips, canoeing, 4x4 trips, water-skiing, sailing, kite-surfing and underwater photography.

🏖 Day Off
Visit the sand dunes at Playa de Las Amoladeras used in various feature films. Also the film studios at Mini Hollywood, remnants from Serge Leone's' spaghetti westerns. Go to the secluded beaches between San Jose and San Miguel and the charming Agua Amarga.

⚙ Best Riding Times

J F M A M J J A S O N D

IT IS AN IDEAL PLACE TO MEANDER ALONG THE COAST STOPPING OFF FOR A COOLING SWIM IN ONE OF THE SECLUDED COVES

CABO DE GATA **RIDES**

Ride 1: La Vela Blanca

↔ 28km

⧗ ¾ day

🍴 ■

💧 ■

⛺ ☺

GPS points

N	W
1. *N36 43 529*	*W002 11 559*
2. *N36 43 628*	*W002 10 628*
3. *N36 45 356*	*W002 06 967*

Start from El Cabo De Gata village. Head along the coastal road through the little village of Almadraba de Montaleva. Just after this town, ignore the right turn to the beach and village at Fabriquilla. Follow the road uphill and around the headland towards Cabo de Gata point. When the road descends look for the dusty vehicle track at the bottom of the hill on the left of the road (GPS 1). Turn down this and follow the track parallel with the coast. After 1.7km you reach a barrier and crude car park (GPS 2). Go through the barrier and ascend to the Cerro De La Vela Blanca viewpoint overlooking the sea. Continue for about 7km to the village of San José. You pass various turnings to good beaches (Playas) in particular the 'Cala Des Los Amarillos' (GPS 3) just before San José.

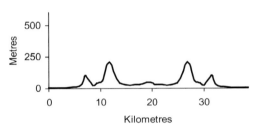

Ride 2: Castillo de San Phillipe

↔ 16.5km

⧗ ¼ day

🍴 ■

💧 ■

⛺ ☺

GPS points

N	W
1. *N36 46 111*	*W002 06 570*
2. *N36 46 149*	*W002 05 824*
3. *N36 48 224*	*W002 03 860*

Start from the village of El Pozo and cycle towards San José on the main road. Just before you reach the village you pass the Hotel El Sotillo on the outskirts of San José. 250m beyond the hotel entrance turn left following signs to Cala Higuera (GPS 1). After 600m continue straight on ignoring the tarmac road, which turns right towards the beach. There is a rough three way junction 600m further on (GPS 2). Take the middle road and head towards the tower on the ridge up ahead in the distance. The track dips down then climbs steeply up and around the headland on a white, loose trail. Follow this coastal track for 11km until you reach the Castillo De San Felipe, a restaurant Casa Emilio and the night-club El Chaman (GPS 3). Join the main road, turn left and follow the road back to El Pozo.

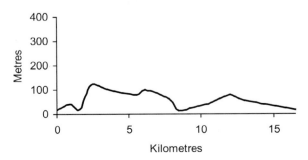

THE DRY SUN BLEACHED
ROCKS STAND IN STARK
CONTRAST TO THE AZURE
MEDITERRANEAN

Ride 3: Ermita del Fraile

 25km

⧖ **¾ day**

GPS points

N	W
1. N36 48 224	W002 03 860
2. N36 48 428	W002 05 078
3. N36 48 942	W002 05 727
4. N36 50 710	W002 06 788
5. N36 50 965	W002 07 313
6. N36 51 489	W002 05 944
7. N36 51 136	W002 02 793

From Rodalquilar follow the main road south passing the Mirador de la Amatista after 2.2km and a turning to La Isleta del Moro after 4.2km. After 6km is a track going to the Castillo de San Felipe and Casa Emilio night-club (GPS 1). Continue on the road as it turns away from the sea. 1.8km further turn right (GPS 2) to the village of Presillas Bajas. In the village is a round, grassy area surrounded by a low wall. Turn left into the little village passing the top edge of this circle. About 150m further is the Finca la Cueta. Turn left downhill and about 350m from the circle is a fenced in electrical sub station by a dry riverbed (GPS 3). Turn right up the riverbed, turning left at a fork after about 1.5km. Follow riverbed trail to Los Albaricoques. About 1km before this town you pass an electrical station (GPS 4) and the trail climbs out of the riverbed and continues on flatter land. At Albaricoques the trail meets the main road (GPS 5), forming a crossroad. Turn right and head for the Ermita Del Fraile. 2.3km from Los Albaricoques go right at a fork (GPS 6) and continue for 6km back to Rodalquilar (GPS 7).

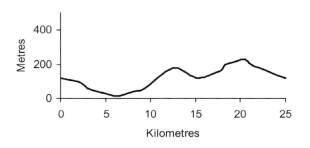

CABO DE GATA RIDES

Ride 4: Volcano Trail

↔ **6km**

⧗ **½ day**

🍴 ■

💧 ■

▦ 🙂

From La Isleta Del Moro head out of town, turn left at the T-junction with the main road and you are heading for the trails that ascend the extinct volcanoes opposite you. 500m along the main road turn right onto the second dusty track you pass and head away from the sea until you climb steeply heading for the large golf ball type structures at the summit. There is a good viewpoint up the La Rellana Mountain and a number of descents to take you back.

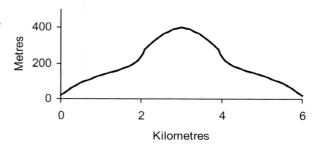

Ride 5: Castillo de San Ramon

↔ **9 km**

⧗ **¼ day**

🍴 ■

💧 ■

▣ ☺

GPS points

N	W
1. *N36 52 339*	*W002 00 203*
2. *N36 51 715*	*W002 00 367*
3. *N36 51 278*	*W002 01 655*

Start from the beach by the La Caleta campsite South of Las Negras. Find the path that goes steeply uphill above the campsite. If you are on the beach facing the sea go to the right-hand side of the beach where the path begins at the edge of the sea (GPS 1). Initially you must carry your bike to the top of the hill then ride the trail around the coast to the next beach 'Playa Del Playazo' where there is a castle 'Castillo de San Ramon' and a large car park (GPS 2). Follow the vehicle track from the car park away from the beach past the 'Castillo De Rodalquilar' until you join the main road (GPS 3). Go right. After 1.7km go right to return to Las Negras.

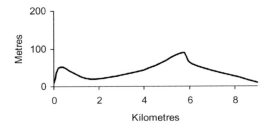

Extension

N	W
1. *N36 53 184*	*W002 00 323*

To develop ride 4 explore the coastal path north of Las Negras that begins at the northern edge of town by a large information board (GPS 1). Follow it to Castillo de San Pedro, Cala de San Pedro, Cala Plomo and Agua Amarga, a relatively large fishing village worth visiting.

CABO DE GATA RIDES

ACCOMMODATION

San José
Hotel Cortijo El Sortillo, 950 611 100.
Hostal Bahía, 950 380 307.
Albergue Juvenile de San José (non-inturjoven youth hostel), 950 380 353.
Camping Tau, 950 380 166 (April - September).

Los Escullos/La Isleta
Hotel Los Escullos, 950 389 733.
Hostal Emilio, 950 389 732.
Camping Los Escullos, 950 389 811 (open all year).

La Isleta
Habitaciones Cortijo La Loma, 950 525 211.
Hostal La Isleta, 950 389 713.

Las Negras
Hostal Arrecife, 950 388 140.
(Lots of holiday apartments).
Camping La Caleta, 950 525 237 (open all year).

Agua Amarga
Hotel Las Calas, 950 138 016.
Hostal La Palmera, 950 138 208.
Hostal Family, 950 138 014.

OTHER AREAS TO EXPLORE

The Alpujarras are relatively close (see Page 168). The hills around Nijar and Turrillas are worthy of exploration.

THE SIERRA NEVADA
AND THE ALPUJARRAS

The Sierra Nevada is a mountain range extending over 2000 km^2 across the southern provinces of Granada and Almería and it is home to Mulhacén (3482m), the highest peak in mainland Spain. There are fourteen other summits over 3000m making these mountains the most elevated massif on the Iberian peninsular. The largest peaks are concentrated in the west near the city of Granada. These huge mountains are part of the extensive Cordillera Bética chain and are still growing at a rate of 0.5mm/year.

The mountains have two protected regions. Whilst the central skeleton of the range is the largest and highest **National** Park in Spain, the slopes forming the surrounding flesh are protected under the **Natural** Park provisions. The upshot of this protected status means that activities within the National Park are carefully controlled. In particular, riding is prohibited on all but vehicle tracks and roads. It is worthy of note that these restrictions are enforced largely to protect people from the mountains rather than the mountains from people. The higher regions are what is called a 'cold desert'; the only water is frozen and very little can live there. Human death is all too common. Activities that involve people straying a long way into the wilderness (such as singletrack mountain bike riding) are strictly monitored because such excursions can so quickly turn to tragedy requiring huge resources to mount rescue operations. The Natural Park area has fewer restrictions and singletrack riding is permissible.

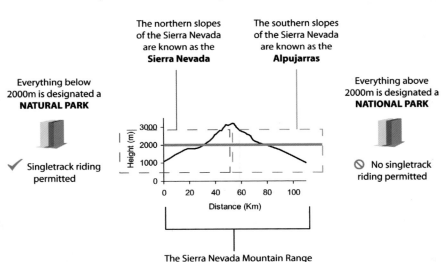

The northern slopes of the Sierra Nevada are known as the **Sierra Nevada**

The southern slopes of the Sierra Nevada are known as the **Alpujarras**

Everything below 2000m is designated a **NATURAL PARK**

✓ Singletrack riding permitted

Everything above 2000m is designated a **NATIONAL PARK**

🚫 No singletrack riding permitted

The Sierra Nevada Mountain Range

We separate this range into two sections. In one we discuss the southern foothills known as the Alpujarras and in the other we talk about the 'Sierra Nevada'. Confusingly this title is used inconsistently to refer to a number of different areas; the National Park, the Natural Park, the ski resort at Pradollano and a massive area encompassing: the valley of Lecrin, the Marquesado del Zenete, the Güéjar-Sierra and the Alpujarras. In our section on 'The Sierra Nevada' we only refer to the area around Granada including the ski resort of Pradollano, the northern foothills below that and the suburbs of Granada (Monachil, Güéjar-Sierra and La Zubia). Although, technically speaking, much of this is not part of the real Sierra Nevada it reflects how the locals refer to the area.

Although the Sierra Nevada and the Alpujarras are neighbouring geographical locations, they are worlds apart in terms of what they have to offer. The Alpujarras are isolated, peaceful and relatively antiquated whilst the Sierra Nevada is accessible, fast, vibrant and racy. Given these differences it is appropriate to deal with them separately. The areas are nonetheless related not least of all because they are joined by one particularly incredible track that crosses the mountain range making it possible to ride from the Alpujarras to Granada.

THE ALPUJARRAS

THE ALPUJARRAS
ANDALUCÍA

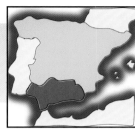

ANDALUCÍA

CÓRDOBA
Córdoba

JAÉN
Jaén

HUELVA

SEVILLA

Huelva ● Sevilla

GRANADA

ALMERÍA

Granada ● Almería

MÁLAGA
CÁDIZ Málaga

Cádiz

Costa de la Luz

Costa del Sol

Costa de Almería

PROVINCE

OF

GRANADA

Baza ●

Guadix ●

Granada ●

Loja ● Güéjar Sierra

Pampaneira ●

15

Lanjarón ●

Almuñécar ● Motril ●

Costa del Sol

THE JAGGED MOUNTAINS ARE
UNIMAGINABLY BEAUTIFUL, INCREDIBLY
REMOTE AND OFFER UNFORGIVING
BUT UNFORGETTABLE RIDING

THE ALPUJARRAS
SOUTHERN SPAIN

Location

The Alpujarras are a 70km long set of deep valleys (barrancos) that form the southern foothills of the Sierra Nevada. They cover 2600 km² half of which fall in the province of Granada and half in Almería. Like the Sierra Nevada Mountains the Alpujarras are higher in the west and gradually decrease the further east you go until they end altogether in the Tabernas desert in Almeria.

General Background

Natural beauty and isolation are the distinguishing features of the Alpujarras. Few roads access the mountains keeping them relatively free from tourism and preserving the old ways of life. Characteristically white labyrinthine villages cling precariously to the hillsides. These complement the natural beauty. The air in the Alpujarras is extremely dry and curing hams and drying chillies are major industries. The Moors occupied the region in the 10th and 11th centuries and the terraced hillsides and canals (acequias) are still visible today. The village of Trevélez at 1476m is home to the highest campsite in Spain.

The Weather

The temperature in the Alpujarras remains relatively warm compared to the neighbouring Sierra Nevada. However, there can be as much as 15°C difference between the top of the Alpujarras and the wooded valleys below. The weather can be extreme; when it rains it is often torrential, snow engulfs the villages, tremendous winds batter their way down hill and blistering summer temperatures desiccate the lush spring growths. Snow remains on the higher slopes from November to March.

Protected Status

The upper slopes of the Alpujarras are protected as a Natural Park but riding is permitted in all areas. It is not until you venture higher into the Sierra Nevada National Park where riding on footpaths becomes prohibited and you must stick to the vehicle tracks.

Local Dangers

The combination of the dry air, steep gradients and extremely high altitudes makes the riding here particularly demanding on your body. Conditions can change rapidly. Cold winds rush off the high mountains even on the hottest days

Mountain Range
Sierra Nevada, Sistema Penibética, Cordillera Bética.

Highest Peak
Mulhacén 3482m.

Getting There
✈ Malaga (240 km)
Granada (110 km).

None.

Nearest Town/City
Lanjaron & Orgiva/Granada.

Equipment Type

DH FR XC

Recommended Bases
Pampaneira, Bubión, Trevélez.

Tourist Information
Sierra Nevada National Park Office, 958 026 300.
Pampaneira visitor centre, 958 763 127.
Lanjaron Information office, 958 770 282.
www.alpujarras.com.

Ride Guides
Michael at 'Switch-Backs', based in Bubión.
www.switch-backs.com. 958 763 163.

Body Repair
Mountain Rescue, 958 481 052.
Surgeries in Pitres and Órgiva.

LOCATING GOOD TECHNICAL
TRAIL IS THE HARDEST THING,
IF IN DOUBT CHECK OUT
ANY OF THE GR 7 ROUTES

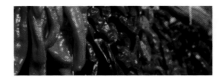

PROS + CONS

+ Insane free-riding
+ Unparalleled natural beauty
+ Long and technical descents
- Dangerous conditions
- Long and steep climbs
- Hard to find trails

requiring you to go prepared for all conditions. The remoteness of the area means that if you get into trouble you could be on your own for a long time so have back up plans.

Equipment

For the long, high vehicle tracks warm cross-country kit and light bikes are what are needed. For the hardcore singletrack, wide thick-treaded tyres are more likely to last; full suspension bikes are the weapons of choice. Padding and robust clothing is essential.

XC Cross-Country

It is a cross-country paradise and teams regularly train on the high peaks. There are plenty of quality vehicle tracks all over the mountains providing long and easy to follow routes.

FR DH Freeride and Downhill

Much of the singletrack descending will challenge the most talented downhill riders. In particular check the GR 7 between Capilerilla and Capileira. There are some superb descents to be found near the Area Recreativa Rio Bermejo running down either side of the Rio Bermejo just above Pórtugos.

Local Observations

Locating good technical trails is the hardest thing. If in doubt check out any of the GR 7 routes. These are well used, well maintained and well marked and are often the best technical trails. If you do spot a trail that looks good, be cautious because it is not unusual for a trail to start well but then turn into something that is too gnarly to continue. Everything about riding in the Alpujarras is ruthless. The uphills are taxing, the altitude is draining, the downhills are demanding, the weather is wearing and even the slashing rocks and sharp, thorny bushes are unforgiving. The singletrack paths are always very steep, very technical and often on the limit of being ride-able. There are sections of such sensationally startling switchbacks littered with gut sucking drop-offs that you will want to ride portions again and again.

Maps 🙂
Editorial Penibética. Parque Nacional Sierra Nevada - Alpujarras, Marquesado del Zenete. Scale - 1:50,000. Buy in tourist information, campsites and shops.

Banks 😐
Most large villages have a cash point.

Fuel 🙁
Nr Pampaneira, Pórtugos, Cádiar.

Bike Repair 😵
No local bike shops. Local mechanics are often worth a go for bodging a bike together if you have no other option. Otherwise a trip to Granada is necessary:See shops Pg 181

Bike Hire 😵

Other Activities 👍
Hiking, horse riding.

Day Off
Very little in the immediate vicinity of this remote region. Granada and the Alhambra Palace are worth a day trip. The Mediterranean beaches are close enough to enjoy.

Best Riding Times

J F M A M J J A S O N D

THE ALPUJARRAS RIDES

Ride 1: Berchules to Timar

20km

½ day

GPS points

N	W
1. N36 58 220	W003 11 440
2. N36 57 910	W003 11 446
3. N36 57 691	W003 11 415
4. N36 57 605	W003 11 170
5. N36 56 733	W003 10 921
6. N36 55 789	W003 11 196
7. N36 55 578	W003 12 009
8. N36 55 850	W003 12 847
9. N36 56 656	W003 12 666
10. N36 57 506	W003 11 740
11. N36 57 836	W003 11 898

Start in the village of Berchules. Take the main road to Alcutar. At this village ignore the right turn into 'Centro Polblacion' and pass a small mini-market on your right. The main road goes around a sharp left-hand bend. Descend for 400m then turn right onto a small concrete road (GPS 1). Descend for 550m to a small hump in the track (GPS 2). Go straight over and descend steeply on the GR 7 for Narilla. After 450m go straight on at a crossroads (GPS 3) continuing on singletrack to the river Cadiar. Follow this downstream for a few hundred metres to a ford (GPS 4). Cross it and go right into Narila. Go through this village and stay on the road for 1km to the next town - Cadiar. At the first fork on the edge of Cadiar turn right. Wiggle through town keeping to the right hand side of town until you reach a large concrete area with a spring in it. Just beyond here a bridge with green railings crosses the river (GPS 5). Go 90m downstream from the bridge and cross the river joining the GR footpath on the far bank. Follow this track downstream for 1.6km then look for the obscure right turning indicated by GR markers (GPS 6). Follow this trail away from the river for 450m to a crossroads by a ruin. Go straight over. Ascend for 1km on technical trail. At the summit (GPS 7) go straight over the crossroads and descend into the next river valley (Rambla Albayar). At the bottom follow the GR footpath out of the riverbed to Lobras. Follow the main road uphill through this village. On the far side, the last building you pass on your right is a small fenced in house with few windows. Turn left opposite this onto a GR marked route (GPS 8). Descend on singletrack to a stream. Cross it and follow an obscure very tough GR route uphill to the village of Timar. From the town spring in Timar (GPS 9) follow the main road for 1km to the first major junction. Go left. 1.4km down hill the road becomes a dirt track. Ignore the first left opposite a farm and continue for 450m to a fork. From here you can see the villages of Cadiar and Nilar below in the distance. Go left. Ignore the first and second right turn and the first left to a quarry. Carry on past a ruin climbing to a building with thin pine trees growing around it. Continue uphill until you pass between rundown buildings built right on the track's edge. In the middle of these buildings turn left (GPS 10). Ascend to a cemetery and the main road (GPS 11). Go right to Berchules.

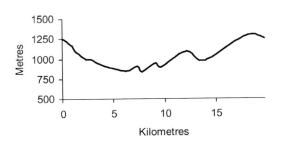

Metres / Kilometres

Ride 2: Mecina-Bombaron to Valor

  19km

  ½ day

GPS points

N	W
1. N36 58 865	W003 09 359
2. N36 58 394	W003 09 073
3. N36 58 109	W003 07 976
4. N36 59 124	W003 07 075
5. N36 59 449	W003 06 729
6. N36 59 481	W003 06 443
7. N36 59 550	W003 05 922

Start in Mecina-Bombaron. Head through the village on the main road towards Yegen. In the middle of town is the town hall on the right where a signboard indicates GR routes. Turn right onto a concrete track descending down the left of the town hall (GPS 1). Follow the GR route from here to the next village - Golco. At Golco turn left at a fork (GPS 2) and 40m downhill follow the GR signposts left to 'Montenegro (50')'. Descend for 400m through steep S-bends to a picnic area where the track levels out. 300m along this flat track turn left onto an obscure singletrack. After 100m it ends at a round platform. Descend off this flat area to the right on a singletrack for 100m down to a vehicle track. Turn left and follow it to Rio de Mecina - a stream. Cross the bridge and follow singletrack on the far side for 1.5km until it ends at a T-junction (GPS 3). Turn left and follow the track to Yegen. Go through this town to the main road between Mecina-Bombaron and Valor. Turn right on this main road. Just as you leave Yegen pass a building on the left called Alojamientos Rurales "Las Eras" (GPS 4). 1.2km from here you pass a large lay-by on the right on a bend in the road. 150m past this turn right onto the marked GR singletrack (GPS 5).

570m downhill you pass a ruin (GPS 6). Descend for 1km to a picnic area and join the tarmac road below it. Turn left uphill for 650m to a left-hand bend in the road where you turn right onto a vehicle track (GPS 7). Follow this track for 250m to a fork. Go left to Valor. After 650m is a T-junction. Go left to the main road. From Valor use the main road to return to Mecina-Bombaron.

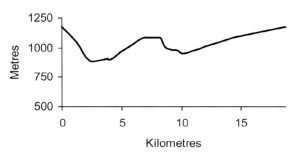

THE ALPUJARRAS RIDES

Ride 3: Capilerilla to Bubión

↔ **13.5km**

⧖ **½ day**

▼ ■

◌ ■

▣ ☹

GPS points

	N	W
1.	N36 56 412	W003 19 796
2.	N36 56 462	W003 20 105
3.	N36 56 315	W003 20 784
4.	N36 56 392	W003 20 993
5.	N36 56 425	W003 20 991
6.	N36 56 823	W003 21 264
7.	N36 56 967	W003 20 813
8.	N36 57 058	W003 20 578
9.	N36 56 848	W003 19 470

Take the GR route between Capilerilla (not Capileira) and Bubión. To find it, follow the road into Capilerilla until it ends at some houses. Take the middle path between the tightly packed buildings passing under concrete roofing. Almost immediately turn right and follow a fence for 50m to a T-junction where wooden GR posts send you right to Bubión (GPS 1). Follow the fairly flat path for 300m until the GR path turns right steeply uphill. Push your bike for about 100m up to a vehicle track. Continue uphill past rusty angle iron fence posts for another 100m and turn right at the next junction. Continue on to a very steep bank. Walk up this and at the top continue uphill to a T-junction with a major vehicle track (GPS 2). Turn left. After 1km you reach a major crossroads (GPS 3). Go straight on (left is signed for 'Cortijo Prado Toro'). Descend for 200m past concrete culverts on the right. 50m further turn right and ascend steeply to a crossroads (GPS 4). Go straight over climbing 50m to the crest of a ridge overlooking Bubión (GPS 5). Descend on singletrack to Bubión. Turn right on the main road at Bubión (GPS 6). Pass through Capileira. Pass a picnic site (2.45km from Bubión) and a vehicle track signed for Cortijo Prado Toro (GPS 7) after 3.7km and a horse riding centre (5km from Bubión). 1.2km from this is a major left hand bend. Turn right onto the vehicle track signed for 'Area Recreativa Rio Bermejo' (GPS 8). After 1.6km turn right at a fork. 400m further look for an obscure singletrack on the right indicated by a cairn/pile of stones. Descend on killer switchbacks for 1km to a vehicle track. Do not follow this around to the right. Instead cross the stream straight ahead (GPS 9) and continue on singletrack descending to another vehicle track. Turn right on this and you soon pass a farm. 450m further and you join the tarmac road that returns to Capilerilla.

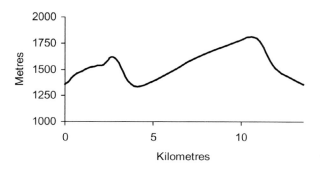

Ride 4: Hoya del Portilla-Capileira

⬌ **22km**

⧗ **¾ day**

🍴 ■

💧 ■

⊡ ☹

GPS points

N	W
1. *N3658 122*	*W003 19 966*
2. *N3656 848*	*W003 19 470*

10.5km above Capileira there is a large car park at the Area Recreativa Hoya del Portillo where there is a manned barrier across the vehicle track to stop vehicles entering the Sierra Nevada National Park (GPS 1). Turn right into the woods at this barrier. After a few hundred metres turn right down a small path and descend to a vehicle track. Go right then first left to continue the singletrack descent. You join the vehicle track going to the Area Recreativa Rio Bermejo (part of ride 3). Go left for a few hundred metres then descend on the obscure singletrack descending into the woods (the top of this trail is marked by a cairn). After 1km you reach a stream (GPS 2). Cross it and descend to a vehicle track. Go right for Capilerilla. From here follow ride 3 to return to Capileira.

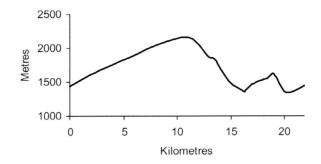

THE ALPUJARRAS RIDES

⬌ **38km**

⧗ **1 day (one way)**

🍴 ◼

💧 ◼

🔲 🙂

GPS points

N	W
1. N36 58 122	*W003 19 966*

Ride 5: Over the top - the highest ride in Spain

10.5km above Capileira is the large car park and visitor centre at the Area Recreativa Hoya del Portillo. This marks the beginning of the Sierra Nevada National Park. Starting from the manned barrier at this car park (GPS 1) it is possible to follow the vehicle track up to the highest point in the Sierra Nevada Mountains before descending to the Prodallano ski resort and eventually crossing the entire Sierra Nevada. The climb is relatively easy allowing access to impressive heights. You can park at the barrier and cycle over to the Granada side of the mountains. It is a dangerous crossing due to a number of factors including the altitude, weather and isolation. As a result you must be well prepared and allow plenty of time. It is advisable to arrange accommodation on the far side and spend the night before returning to the start point.

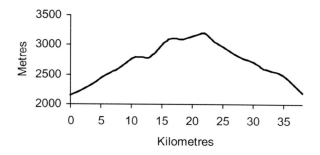

ACCOMMODATION

Pampaneira
P* Pampaneira, 958 763 002.
P* Ruta del Mulhacen, 958 763 010.

Bubión
HA*** Villa Turística Del Poqueira, 958 763 111.
P** Terrazas de la Alpujarra, 958 763 252.

Trevélez
H* La Fragua, 958 858 573.
P* Fernando, 958 858 565.
P* Regina, 958 858 564.
Camping Trevélez 2a (open all year), 958 858 735.

OTHER AREAS TO EXPLORE

The GR route between Trevélez and Busquístar is worth exploring. You can either ride over to or drive to the Sierra Nevada and Granada. Plenty of riding there worth visiting.

SIERRA NEVADA

SIERRA NEVADA
GRANADA - ANDALUCÍA

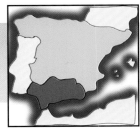

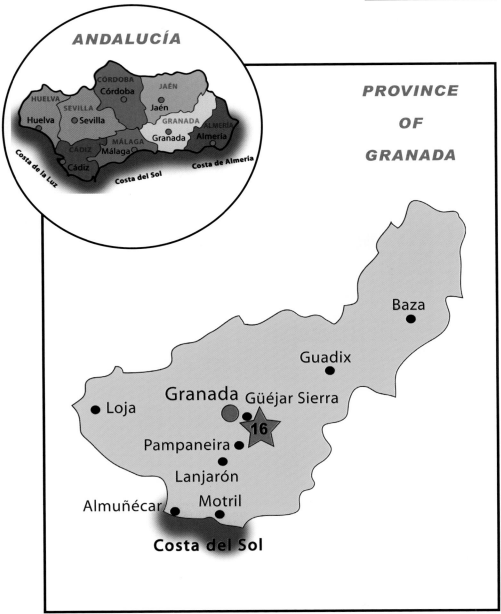

ANDALUCÍA

HUELVA
Huelva
SEVILLA
Sevilla
CÓRDOBA
Córdoba
JAÉN
Jaén
GRANADA
Granada
ALMERÍA
Almería
MÁLAGA
Málaga
CÁDIZ
Cádiz
Costa de la Luz
Costa del Sol
Costa de Almería

PROVINCE
OF
GRANADA

Baza
Guadix
Granada
Güéjar Sierra
16
Loja
Pampaneira
Lanjarón
Motril
Almuñécar
Costa del Sol

RARELY DO YOU FIND SO VAST A NATURAL WILDERNESS ON THE DOORSTEP OF SUCH A LIVELY CITY; PLENTY OF FUN TO BE HAD ON OR OFF YOUR BIKE

SIERRA NEVADA
SOUTHERN SPAIN

Location

Everything about the Sierra Nevada mountain range is massive; it covers over 2000km², spans two counties - Granada and Almeria - and nearly one fifth of its peaks are over 3000 metres high. For the purposes of this section we focus on a relatively small part of this huge range: the mountains and foothills around the city of Granada. In particular we cover the Pradollano ski resort the Sierra Nevada Natural Park and the suburbs surrounding Granada - Monachil, Güéjar-Sierra and La Zubia. This is the most developed region in the mountain range and the regular visitors mean that there is an abundance of well-used and well-maintained trails.

General Background

Granada is famous for the Alhambra Palace that was a spectacular pleasure dome during Moorish times. You can tour the grounds but there are hordes of visitors throughout the year so visit early. Flamenco music and dancing is popular and the city's fiestas involve days of hardcore partying in the streets when absolutely everyone joins in. The city's seductiveness is in part due to the fact that from practically anywhere you can see the snow capped peaks of the Sierra Nevada. Despite a colorful history Granada is not stuck in the past. Extreme sports of all kinds find their home here. A lively young population punctuates nocturnal frivolities with all manner of mountain madness.

The Weather

Although the region's climate is classified as 'Mediterranean', the high mountains create insane microclimates. The high peaks are intensely cold in the winter and hot and dry in the summer. In fact the higher reaches are classed as a cold desert. The summer falls quite precisely into July and August. September sees the beginnings of autumn and the first snows usually arrive in October. From about the end of March spring comes thick and fast; the area is sunny and green for a few months before being desiccated by the summer heat.

Protected Status

The highest mountains are protected as a National Park where mountain biking is restricted. You can only ride on roads and vehicle tracks in this zone and no singletrack riding is permitted. There are two exceptions to this rule. The ski resort at Pradollano is open for riders to use in the summer. The second area is a purpose built World Cup cross-country circuit just outside of Pradollano. The restrictions apply to save lives not the mountains. The lower slopes are protected as a Natural Park and riding is permitted in most places.

Mountain Range
Sierra Nevada, Sistema Penibética, Cordillera Bética.

Highest Peak
Mulhacén 3482m.

Getting There
Málaga (125km), Alicante (351 km),Madrid (423km). Granada (20km).

Nearest Town/City
Güéjar-Sierra/*Granada (20km).*

Equipment Type

XC   DH   FR

Recommended Bases
Güéjar-Sierra, Penos Genil, La Zubia and Monachil.

Tourist Information
Granada Tourist Office, Tel: 958 225 990.
Centro De Visitantes El Dornajo
(10km before Pradollano ski station).

Ride Guides
Exodus (www.exodus.co.uk).
Sierra Nevada club (www.sierranevadaski.com, bikearea@cetursa.es).

Body Repair
Cruz Roja, 958 222 222. Granada Hospital, 958 241 724.
Mountain Rescue, 958 481 052.

AFTER A FREE-RIDE FIESTA AND
SOME SUBURBAN RIDGE RIDING, HIT
THE CITY'S BARS AND ABSORB THE
BEER, HOSPITALITY AND FREE TAPAS

Local Dangers

Being stranded in these mountains can
be perilous at any time of year. Either
the extreme heat or cold will defeat
even the fittest of athletes. The effects
of altitude can be quite draining if you
are not used to the extreme heights.

Equipment

Carry water, clothes, food and
spares for the rides on these
remote and high mountains.

XC Cross-Country

Above the suburb of La Zubia there is
a pinewood full of worthwhile
singletrack and cross-country routes.
Güéjar Sierra has some long climbs
and descents and offers the most

varied riding. The rides around Pradollano include some of the highest in Europe. It is possible to take one vehicle
track and cross the entire mountain range passing under Mulhacén peak before descending down into the Alpujarras.

FR DH Freeride and Downhill

Motor-cross bikes are popular with the city folk and riders have carved some fierce free-ride trails into the suburban
hills around Monachil, Güéjar Sierra and Pinos Genil. These make excellent freeride and downhill routes.

Local Observations

Respect the altitude and sun as both can sap your strength. Carrying sufficient water and the right clothing is crucial.
At any time of year cold gusts of air can blast down off the higher snowy peaks bringing breathtakingly cold air that
can quickly chill you on even the hottest day. Like Monty Pythons' Spanish Inquisition, expect the unexpected.

Maps ☺
Series: Editorial Penibética. Parque Nacional Sierra
Nevada - Alpujarras, Marquesado del Zenete 1:50,000.
Buy in tourist information, campsites and shops.

Banks ☺
Cash points in all towns.

Fuel ☺
Petrol stations on major roads and in towns.

Bike Repair ☺
Bicicletas San Miguel, 18100 Armilla, Av Poniente.
Bicicletas Mam, C/Ribera. 18200, Maracena..
Bicicletas Smar, Centro Commercial Netuno.

Bike Hire ☺

Other Activities
Paragliding, horse riding, skiing, snow-boarding, rock
climbing, mountaineering, fishing, hiking, sight-seeing.

Day Off
Visit the Alhambra Palace and Albyzin and do some
general site seeing around Granada. Watch and even take
part in some Flamenco.

**Best Riding
Times**

J F M A M J J A S O N D

SIERRA NEVADA RIDES

Ride 1: Collada de la Gitana

⬌ **15km**

⌛ **½ day**

🍴 ■

🌢 ■

▣ 😊

GPS points

N	W
1. N37 10 153	W003 23 760
2. N37 10 161	W003 23 043
3. N37 10 380	W003 23 822
4. N37 10 622	W003 23 867
5. N37 10 914	W003 25 082
6. N37 10 775	W003 25 883
7. N37 10 501	W003 26 494
8. N37 09 844	W003 26 670

From Güéjar-Sierra ascend to the Balderas campsite (GPS 1). 1.2km past the entrance turn left (GPS 2). After 1.3km you reach the summit of this climb (GPS 3) called the Collado de la Gitana pass. At the peak follow the track around a right-hand bend and it starts to descend gently. After 100m, leave the main track and find the singletrack on your left (initially hard to spot). After about 500m it goes over a rise (GPS 4) and descends for 2km to a farm (GPS 5). Join the track in front of the farm and follow it for 750m until a track joins you from the right. Ignore this and go straight on for a further 800m until another track joins you from the right; ignore this too. A small track joins from the left at (GPS 6) just after which there is a big white house on the right. 1.2km from this house you reach a sign posted junction (GPS 7). Ignore the right to 'Cjo Argamosa and Quéntar'. Go straight on back to Güéjar-Sierra (GPS 8).

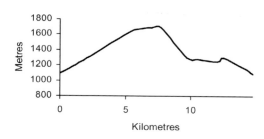

Ride 2: Alto de Calar

⬌ **17km**

⌛ **½ day**

🍴 ■

🌢 ■

▣ ☹

GPS points

N	W
1. N37 10 380	W003 23 897
2. N37 10 775	W003 25 883
3. N37 10 272	W003 26 626
4. N37 09 844	W003 26 670

Follow ride 3 to the top of the ascent at the Collado de la Gitana pass just above the Balderas Campsite. This time instead of going around the bend at the top, head towards the peak of the mountain where a small red/brown path can be seen going to the summit. This path becomes better defined about 100m from the bend at GPS 1. Follow the tricky trail along the ridge of the mountain created by motor-cross bikes heading for the peak called 'Alto de Calar' (1878m). You pass old bunkers near this peak and a long descent begins basically following a series of electrical pylons. At the bottom you join a vehicle track (GPS 2). Turn left and immediately pass a white house on your right. Go left for 1.3km until you reach a sign posted junction (GPS 3). Go straight on and you reach Güéjar-Sierra after about 2.5km (GPS 4).

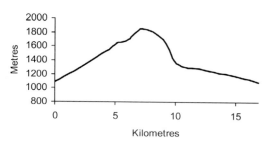

Ride 3: Loma de Los Jarales

 Variable

 Variable

As you travel from Pinos Genil to Güéjar-Sierra there is a ridge of mountains on your left called Loma de Los Jarales. About 800m from the start of this road you pass a bus shelter on the right opposite which there is a concrete road. Follow it steeply up (GPS 1) to find a multitude of trails along the ridges of these hills.

GPS points

N	W
1. *N37 09 857*	*W003 30 008*

Ride 4: Quéntar via Fuente Teja

 Variable

 Variable

From camping Las Lomos in Güéjar-Sierra turn right and take the first left turn onto a minor road. Follow it steeply uphill for about 600m until you stop climbing following a small sign to Fuente Teja (GPS 1). A vehicle track begins by this bank of springs. Follow it to a sign-posted junction at (GPS 2). Follow the signs to Quéntar and keep heading for the lake.

GPS points

N	W
1. *N37 09 844*	*W003 26 670*
2. *N37 10 501*	*W003 26 494*

SIERRA NEVADA RIDES

8km

Variable

Ride 5: Pradollano World Cup Circuit

The purpose built cross-country World Cup Circuit is found about ¾ km before you reach the Pradollano Ski Resort on the left of the A395 main road. There is a junction where another road joins on the left and there is a large parking area with a section of an old bubble car. The ride is in the woods at this road junction.

Variable

Variable

Monachil

A down-hilling playground exists near the paragliding take off point on the mountains called Cerro de Loma Redonda and Cerro del Grajo. From Monachil follow the road out of town towards the Ski station going over a river bridge in town (GPS 1). After 4.1km pass the restaurant 'Merendero Fuente La Miguita' (GPS 2). 700m from here turn left onto a vehicle track (GPS 3) where a variety of descents begin.

GPS points

N	W
1. N37 07 946	W003 32 349
2. N37 08 245	W003 30 486
3. N37 08 386	W003 30 184

Variable

Variable

La Zubia

Just above La Zubia the 'Cumbrias Verdes (green fields) start on the edge of town (GPS 1). Go 4km uphill from town heading for the Botanical Gardens at 'Mirador Del Trevenque y Sierra Nevada'. At a junction by the restaurant La Guitarra (GPS 2) go left. 600m on is a lay-by (GPS 3) where a singletrack descent begins in the woods. Alternatively keep climbing to the Mirador.

GPS points

N	W
1. N37 06 914	W003 34 666
2. N37 05 737	W003 32 556
3. N37 05 609	W003 32 230

OTHER AREAS TO EXPLORE

ALPUJARRAS
The Alpujarras are relatively close and worth a visit (see previous section). You can drive or take the long ride over the top of the Sierra Nevada. To cross the range take the road past the Ski resort at Pradollano, under the Veleta peak (3394m) to Carihuela. It eventually drops down into Capileira in the Alpujarras where there are plenty of places to stay. A full days ride only to be considered in good weather.

DILAR
In Dilar a vehicle track begins by a small red Moorish castle that heads to Padul. Small posts saying 'Cuo Padul' and 'Silleta del Padul' mark the way.

ACCOMMODATION

Granada

There is the range of accommodation that you would expect to find in a city of Granada's size and stature. Here are just a few.

Camping Los Álamos, Carretera de Málaga, km 400, Granada, Tel 958 208 479.
Camping María Eugenia, Avenida Andalucia 190, Granada, Tel: 958 200 606.
Camping Sierra Nevada, Carretera de Jaén 107, Granada, Tel: 958 150 062.

Guejar Sierra

Camping Las Lomas, 1a, 958 484 742.
Log cabins available (open all year). Lovely setting with excellent facilities.

La Zubia

Camping Reina Isabel 3a,
www.campingreinaisabel.com, 958 590 041 (open all year). Has an excellent restaurant worth visiting even if you are not staying there.

ARDARLES NATURAL PARK

SIERRA DE ARDARLES
MÁLAGA - ANDALUCÍA

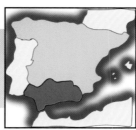

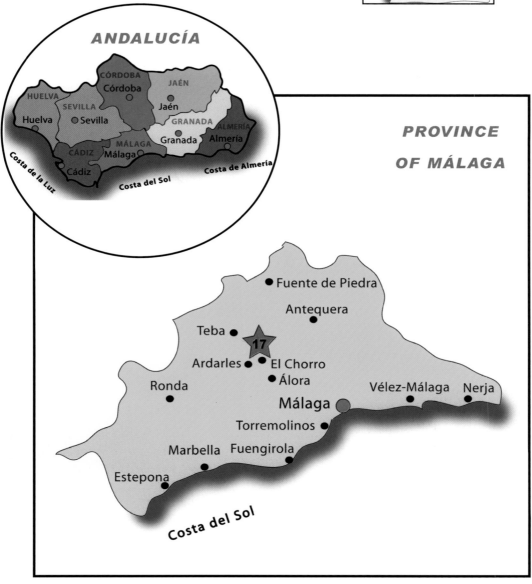

ANDALUCÍA

HUELVA
Huelva

SEVILLA
Sevilla

CÓRDOBA
Córdoba

JAÉN
Jaén

GRANADA
Granada

ALMERÍA
Almería

CÁDIZ
Cádiz

MÁLAGA
Málaga

Costa de la Luz

Costa del Sol

Costa de Almería

PROVINCE

OF MÁLAGA

Fuente de Piedra

Antequera

Teba

17

Ardarles

El Chorro

Álora

Ronda

Vélez-Málaga

Nerja

Málaga

Torremolinos

Marbella

Fuengirola

Estepona

Costa del Sol

ARDARLES NATURAL PARK
SOUTHERN SPAIN

Location

The riding focuses around the small village of El Chorro. This sleepy village is 15km north of Álora and 50km north of Málaga. Although close to the sprawling coast, the deep gorge and winding mountain roads preserve the town from invasion. Furthermore, much of the land around the village is either too steep to support major development or is protected by being within the Ardales Natural Park. Consequently these beautiful mountain slopes are certain to remain unspoiled well into the future. The sheer walls of La Huma Mountain overlook El Chorro. These cliffs create the walls of the astonishing gorge called 'Desfiladero De Los Gaitanes' - the village's centrepiece.

General Background

The Guadalhorce River flows through this dramatic gorge and explains El Chorro's name which, literally translated means 'an outpouring of water'. This famous natural phenomenon is so impressive it is featured in practically any Spanish walking book. It is 3km long, 400m deep but often only 10m wide. An incredible Indiana Jones style walkway called the 'Camino Del Rey' clings to the walls of the canyon but this is currently closed. The fantastic rocky scenery that makes the area so alluring is the result of limestone beds that have been lifted to near vertical. To say the area is popular with rock-climbers is an understatement and El Chorro is home to the National Climbing School. At the opposite end of the gorge are the

startlingly turquoise reservoirs that provide water for much of Málaga province. There are a couple of excellent restaurant/bars around the dam wall that separate the three main reservoirs Embalses Del Guadalteba, Del Guadalhorce and Del Conde De Guadalhorce.

The Weather

Heavy rain and bad weather are confined to a few short winter months. Often this 'wet season' is disappointingly dry and droughts are common. Spring comes early and for March, April and May the mountains are incredibly verdant. Summer is intense when temperatures rarely leave the 40°C mark. Autumn is a repeat of spring as the first rains revive the scorched landscape.

Protected Status

Riding is permitted within the Ardales Natural Park consequently you are not prohibited from riding anywhere.

Local Dangers

The peak summer heat makes riding inadvisable because any strenuous activity means it's impossible to keep up with the rate at which your body consumes water. Snakes are common. The big ones are OK, watch out for the small, thin, black ones which may be semi-poisonous vipers.

Mountain Range
Sierra Del Chorro, Sistema Penibético, Cordillera Bética.

Highest Peak
La Huma 1191m.

Getting There
Málaga Airport (50km), Seville (207km).
El Chorro, Álora (15km).

Nearest Town/City
Álora (15km)/*Málaga (50km)*.

Equipment Type
FR   XC

Recommended Bases
El Chorro.

Tourist Information
Tourist office Álora, Avda. De la Constitución, s/n, 952 498 380.

Ride Guides
Olive-Works, www.olive-works.net.
Swiss owned Finca La Campana, 952 112 019.

Body Repair
Álora - emergencies, 952 496 088

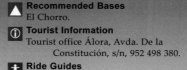

RIDE, REFUEL AND REST IN
EL CHORRO, THE HEART OF
THE PICTURE POSTCARD
SPANISH LAKE DISTRICT

☑ Equipment

The steep uphills make you wish you had a light cross-country bike but the demented descents make you wish for something big and bouncy. Either full-suspension cross-country bikes or a free-ride bike will be at home. Good water carrying equipment is essential because it is dry, high and hot.

XC Cross-Country

There are countless long, dusty vehicle tracks to explore with long undulating ascents and descents. Locals are laid back and cycling across their land is not an issue though some of the farmers' dogs are quite territorial.

DH Downhill

Good downhill routes can be found from the La Mesa reservoir.

FR Freeride

The finest playground is the pinewood above El Chorro village. This is just behind the campsite and you will find networks of singletrack and vehicle track on a steep wooded slope. The climbers who wander up and down to access climbing locations keep these paths well trodden.

👁 Local Observations

This destination is one of the few places where a car is not essential. You can fly into Malaga, catch a train to El Chorro and practically fall out of the train into a well-equipped campsite at the base of the best rides. Cycling through the phenomenal rock formations on skinny, virgin trails infused with heady pine fragrances can cause a sensory overload. You will have to exert yourself on the 'ups' but the 'downs' will astound you. You can then rest at a lakeside retreat and feast on their endless menus that won't empty your pockets. The diversity of different trail types is impressive. There are wooded singletracks, insane rocky descents and undulating vehicle tracks that go on for miles - something to please everyone. If you look south-west towards Ardales from the top of the La Mesa Mountain there are a multitude of trails covering the hills below that can offer superb riding.

Paraje
Natural

Maps 😟
Mapa Cartografía Militar De España. 1:50 000, 16-43 (1038) 'Ardales'. By in the Refugio in El Chorro or Corte Inglés in Málaga,Marbella or Estepona.

Banks 😟
Álora & Valle de Abdalajis.

Fuel 😟
Álora & Valle de Abdalajis.

Bike Repair 😀
Estrada Recambios, Avda. De Cervantes, 19, Álora (for basic spares).
Bike Station Marbella,Ntra. Sra. De Gracia 11, 952 861 807.

OW OLIVEWORKS

Bike Hire 😀
Finca La Campana, 952 112 019. Camping El Chorro, Estación de El Chorro, 952 112 696.

Other Activities
Hiking, rock-climbing, paragliding, canoeing, fishing, ornithology, pedaloes, wind surfing, horse riding.

Day Off
Explore the ancient Bobastro ruins. Learn to rock climb in El Chorro. Visit Ronda and its famous bull ring and bridge. The Costa Del Sol is 45 minutes away.

Best Riding Times

■■■■■■■■■■■■
J F M A M J J A S O N D

WOODED SINGLETRACK, INSANE
ROCKY DESCENTS AND UNDULATING
VEHICLE TRACKS CAN ALL BE
FOUND PACKED INTO THIS AREA

EL CHORRO RIDES

Ride 1: The Sierra Llana - El Kiosco to the El Gaitenejo Sub Station

↔ **5km**

⧗ **¼ day**

🍴 ▨

🛢 ▨

⬚ ☺

GPS points

N	W
1. N36 55 946	W004 48 105
2. N36 55 951	W004 47 365
3. N36 55 871	W004 47 961

Start at the restaurant 'El Kiosco' on the edge of the 'Embalse Del Conde de Guadalhorce' reservoir. As you look at the restaurant, go through the tunnel on the right hand side of the building. On the far side of the tunnel turn right onto singletrack (GPS 1). You descend to the river then follow the trail for 2km until you reach the electrical sub station 'El Gaitenejo' (GPS 2). At the sub station go right up the vehicle track that soon goes through another tunnel after a few hundred metres. 1.6km uphill from the substation is a barrier (GPS3). Turn right towards the viewpoint. A few hundred metres uphill you can see the viewpoint coming into view to your left. Carry on past it to the right. Although the vehicle track you are on seems to end, there is a steep but obscure singletrack descent through the trees that rejoins the trail you rode at the start of the ride. Join it near the top of the descent and turn left so that you retrace your steps back to the tunnel by El Kiosco restaurant.

Ride 2: Cerro de la Cueva and Loma del Pajarero to Ardales

↔ **18km**

⧗ **¾ day**

🍴 ■

🛢 ▨

⬚ ☺

GPS points

N	W
1. N36 54 725	W004 47 214
2. N36 54 280	W004 46 620
3. N36 52 554	W004 48 488
4. N36 52 545	W004 49 350
5. N36 52 812	W004 50 279
6. N36 54 851	W004 48 427

Head out of El Chorro towards Ardales on the main road. Follow the same directions as ride 3 taking the turning signed to Bobastro Ruins about 4km from town (GPS 1). Instead of ascending to the summit of La Mesa, this time only ascend for 2.5km until the road levels off briefly and there is a lay-by on your right where a GR route begins (GPS 2). Turn onto this dusty track and follow it for 4.6km. Although there are numerous junctions the correct route is always obvious because red and white markers indicate the correct direction or there are chains and barriers preventing you from taking the wrong route. Some incorrect routes are quite obviously just driveways to people's homes. There is a very steep descent followed by a very difficult climb that eventually ends at a minor tarmac road (GPS 3). Turn left onto this road and follow it towards Ardales. After 1.7km you reach the summit of a short climb and Ardales comes into view below you (GPS 4). Descend towards it until the track ends at a T-junction next to the major A357 main road (GPS 5). Go underneath this fast road and follow the road signs back to El Chorro. You ride for about 7km along the road with the Embalse Del Conde de Guadalhorce on your left until you reach a right turn (GPS 6). Turn right here to return to El Chorro.

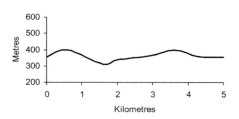

Ride 3: Tajo de la Encantada - the La Mesa Descent

13km

½ day

GPS points

N	W
1. N36 54 725	W004 47 214
2. N36 54 044	W004 46 690
3. N36 54 357	W004 46 539
4. N36 54 280	W004 46 620
5. N36 54 423	W004 45 857

Take the main road out of El Chorro in the direction of Ardales. Cross the dam wall/bridge just below the village. Turn right at the T-junction on the far side of this bridge and follow the road keeping the El Chorro reservoir on your right. Follow the road towards the gorge. You pass hydroelectric turbines on your right after a few hundred metres and about 700m further a bar on your left. After a total of 2km from town the road swings sharply left just as you reach the gorge. Continue for 1.8km from the gorge and take the first left turn sign posted to the 'Bobastro' Ruins (GPS 1). This road ascends steeply for 4km up the La Mesa Mountain to a reservoir at the top (GPS 2). (There is a bar if you follow the main road past the reservoir until it ends). Turn right on the service road around the reservoir and follow it anticlockwise to the far side (1.4km) where you turn right and descend down a slip road (GPS 3) for 200m. As soon as the slip road stops descending steeply look to your left and locate the (difficult to see) left turn into the woods (GPS 4). Follow this GR marked route and descend on a progressively treacherous, rocky track all the way back down until you come out by the power station turbines opposite El Chorro village (GPS 5).

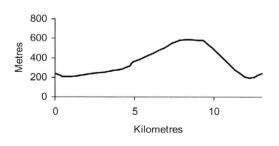

EL CHORRO RIDES

Ride 4: Sierra de Huma Pinewood Singletrack

↔ **10km**

⧗ **½ day**

GPS points

N	W
1. N36 54 433	W004 45 534
2. N36 54 816	W004 45 147
3. N36 55 044	W004 44 318
4. N36 54 896	W004 44 318
5. N36 54 652	W004 44 815
6. N36 54 770	W004 45 125

Start at the El Chorro train station (GPS 1) and head away from the Garganta Hotel/Restaurant, through a residential area. After 100m you pass between two galvanised pylons very close together. Follow the path uphill towards the woods. After 265m there is a T-junction with a track. Go left (you can see the back of the campsite ahead). After 80m turn right uphill into the woods on a vehicle track signed to 'Haza Del Rio'. Follow this track for 1.7km until you pass a track on your left with a barrier across it and signed 'Precaucion Colmenas' ('Caution Bees') (GPS 6). Ignore it for now. 80m beyond this turn right (GPS 2) up a steep track. 500m uphill is a rough junction. Follow the track to the left. 2km from here you reach the top of the woods. A white house with white gravel drive can be seen behind the last trees (GPS 3). With this building behind so you are looking downhill, turn left and follow the track along the top edge of the woods to the far left-hand side of the pinewood. At the fork (GPS 4) turn right so that you descend down the left-hand side of the woods. After 300m the track becomes singletrack. There are a couple of minor junctions. At each one stay as close as possible to the ridge on the left until the singletrack climbs up the side of this ridge to some derelict buildings (GPS 5) at the summit. Go right along the spine of the ridge following the path 800m from the ruins until it rejoins the vehicle track you originally ascended. Go right, back uphill for 460m returning to the track on the left with a barrier that you noted earlier (GPS 6). Turn down this track. Carefully pass a number of bee hives. Singletrack resumes just after the hives and takes you back down to the village.

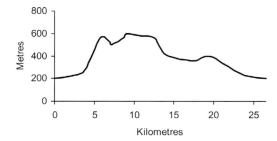

OTHER AREAS TO EXPLORE

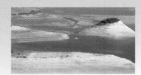

Ronda is relatively close and boasts a host of different riding locations. Near Benalmadena Costa there is a télecabina cable car ascending the Tivoli Mountain. You can take this up the mountain to enjoy effortless descents.

IN THIS RIDING DESTINATION
YOU WILL HAVE TO EXERT
YOURSELF ON THE 'UPS' BUT THE
'DOWNS' WILL BE WELL WORTH IT

ACCOMMODATION

El Chorro
Olive-Works, www.olive-works.net.
Hotel/Apartments La Garganta, 952 495 119.
Finca La Campana, 952 112 019.
Pension Estación, 952 495 004.
Camping El Chorro, 952 112 696.

Las Angosturas
Rocabella, Alojamientos Rurales, Las Angosturas. Expensive, but classy houses to rent
with private swimming pool just outside El Chorro. Book well in advance.

Lakes/Reservoirs
***Posada de Conde, 952 112 411.
Camping Ardales, 952 458 120.

SIERRA DE GRAZALEMA

SIERRA DE GRAZALEMA
CÁDIZ - ANDALUCÍA

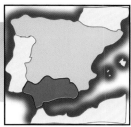

ANDALUCÍA

HUELVA
SEVILLA
CÓRDOBA
JAÉN
GRANADA
ALMERÍA
MÁLAGA
CÁDIZ

Huelva
Sevilla
Córdoba
Jaén
Granada
Almería
Málaga
Cádiz

Costa de la Luz
Costa del Sol
Costa de Almería

PROVINCE
OF CÁDIZ

Sanlúcar de Barrameda
Jerez de la Frontera
Arcos de la Frontera
18 Grazalema
Rota
El Puerto de Santa Maria
San Fernando
Medina - Sidonia
Cornil de la Frontera
Barbate
San Roque
Algeciras
La Línea de la Concepción
Tarifa

Costa de la Luz

SIERRA DE GRAZALEMA

EASTERN SPAIN

Location

The Grazalema Natural Park straddles Malaga and Cadiz provinces covering about 500 km^2 making it fairly small by Andalucian standards. The town that gives its name to the park, Grazalema, is a little over 100km from the Costa del Sol but it can take many hours to travel between the two due to the painfully slow roads. Driving between the towns of Grazalema and Zahara is a treacherous but inspiring experience as you cross through the 'Puerto de Los Palomas' mountain pass (1331m).

General Background

The area remained a Moorish strong hold to the end of the Catholic/Moorish conflicts in the 14th century. Most modern towns are based upon the remains of impregnable ancient fortresses. Many still retain the 'De La Frontera' affix, which is a name given to towns that were on the front line during this war. As the battle lines moved to and fro, towns fell and were retaken by both sides. Ronda is a superb example; an old town built with this classic fortress-like impregnability. Being one of the last places to be conquered, it retains Moorish characteristics better than anywhere in Spain. Isolation is the defining characteristic of the park. Its seclusion and considerable natural beauty means it has developed as a major attraction for nature lovers. The inaccessible peaks and gorges are teeming with rare wildlife, plants and trees. Consequently there are few places in Spain that are as strenuously protected as here and this impacts heavily on where you can ride.

The Weather

Since it receives about 2150mm rainfall per annum, Grazalema has the dubious accolade of being Spain's wettest village. This is a curious fact as it is located in the heart of the notoriously parched province of Andalucia, which is regularly plagued by drought. It can be stormy inside the park whilst just outside regular sunshine abounds. Anytime between November and May can be wet but the summers are long and consistently dry. Winter regularly sees snowfall on the higher mountains.

Protected Status

In the hills just to the south of Zahara there is a 30km^2 area that is seriously protected called the 'Area de Reserva'. The Torreon Peak (1654m) and Garganta Verde are within this area and mountain biking is absolutely prohibited here. In fact, you can only walk in here if you have a permit from the El Bosque Park Office. Europe's largest colony of Griffin Vultures lives in these parts as well as some Golden Eagles.

Local Dangers

Low cloud, narrow mountain roads and wet conditions make driving and cycling around this area treacherous. The exposed limestone rocks that litter the trails can be untrustworthy when wet. Therefore be cautious when riding both on- and off-road.

Mountain Range
Cordillera Bética, Sierra de Grazalema.

Highest Peak
El Pinar (1654m).

Getting There
✈ Málaga (140km).
🚂 Ronda (30km).

Nearest Town/City
Grazalema/*Marbella (85km)*.

Equipment Type
XC   FR

Recommended Bases
Grazalema, Zahara de la Sierra.

Tourist Information
Plaza de España, Grazalema, 956 132 225.

Ride Guides
Al-Qutun, 956 137 882.

Other Activities
Walking, ornithology, canoeing, rock climbing, caving, paragliding & fishing.

THE DOWNHILLS ARE
FULL OF SURPRISES WITH
DECEPTIVELY TRICKY,
ROCKY DROP-OFFS

PROS + CONS
+ Outstanding natural beauty
+ Long, inspiring rides
+ Classic Andalucian villages
- Difficult to locate singletrack
- Highest rainfall in Spain

☑ Equipment

There are a lots of gorse bushes and thorny shrubs requiring good supplies of inner tubes and puncture repair kits. The protective strips that you insert into your tyres can be useful. Thick tyres are a good idea for dealing with the thorns and for the generally tough conditions. Long sleeved light tops can help save your arms from being shredded. Light bikes with travel front and rear are most suited to the varied terrain.

XC Cross-Country

The perilous roads are popular with cross-country riders and, so long as you use these to link some of the vehicle tracks together, it is possible to enjoy rides of immense distances. It is worth considering riding between villages with a credit card and change of clothes so you can take your time meandering through the area.

FR DH Freeride and Downhill

As you climb out of Zahara de la Sierra to the Puerto de Las Palomas pass there is a network of firebreaks on the left of the road that can provide superb descents (mentioned in ride 2).

👁 Local Observations

Grazalema is just a small slice of the riding that is available in the Ronda Valley region, however, it is a particularly attractive slice. The best rides are found around the towns of Benaojan, Grazalema and Zahara. Despite the sizeable chunk of protected land where riding is prohibited, you are free to ride practically anywhere else. The area has a surprisingly similar feel to the Lake District. The wet weather, lakes and green, sheep littered mountains all have an English feel to them but the analogy is developed by the fact that the farmers are armed to the teeth with wellington boots and Land Rovers. The limestone landscape is well weathered by the endless precipitation. This has created ancient networks of well-established watercourses so that even if it does rain, the ground drains quickly and rides are not too boggy. Sample the excellent local pork from the black pigs reared in the area (Lomo Iberico).

Maps 😐
Series: Mapa Guia, Parque Natural Sierra de Grazalema, 1:50,000. Buy in Grazalema.

Banks 😐
Grazalema, Zahara de la Sierra.

Fuel 😞
Grazalema, Ubrique, Cortes de la Frontera.

Bike Repair 😞
Bicicletas Jesus Rosado SL, Plaza del Ahorro, 1, Cte Salvador Carrasco, L1, Ronda, www.acobis.com, Jrosado@ronda.net, 952 870 221.

Bike Hire 😞

Day Off
See the Cueva de la Pileta caves and rock paintings near Benaojan. Walk the Garganta Verde gorge in grazalema Park (you need to get a free permit from tourist offices). Visit the stunning town of Ronda. Go to the beach(between Estepona and Marbella). Take a day trip to Gibraltar.

Best Riding Times

J F M A M J J A S O N D

SIERRA DE GRAZALEMA RIDES

Ride 1: The PR-A 254 Benaojan to Jimera de Líbar

↔ **15km**

⧗ **½ day**

🍴 ⬜

⛽ ⬛

▣ 🙂

GPS points

N	W
1. *N36 42 767*	*W005 14 865*
2. *N36 42 742*	*W005 14 759*

From Benaojan train station cross over the tracks at a small crossing (GPS 1). Then cross the river Guadiaro on the footbridge. On the far bank of the river turn right (GPS 2). Follow signs for PR-A 254 to Jimera de Líbar. Continue along the very technical singletrack that follows the river rising high above it before descending back to the water as you reach Jimera de Líbar. It is possible to continue for approximately 10 km beyond Jimera de Líbar on the river path. Return to the start by taking either the train at 5.33 p.m., the main road on the far side of the river or returning the way you came.

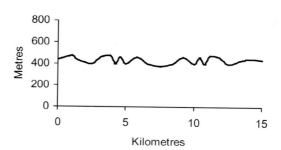

Ride 2: Firebreaks Above the Embalse de Zahara - El Gastor

↔ **12km**

⧗ **½ day**

🍴 ⬜

⛽ ⬛

▣ 😐

GPS points

N	W
1. *N36 48 256*	*W005 23 383*

This is a whole riding area that you can see on the left of the road as you cycle uphill from Zahara on the CA531 towards Grazalema. There is a clearly visible network of firebreaks on these slopes to the left of the road. About 4.3km on the CA 531 from the outskirts of Zahara is a lay-by on the right for the 'Sendero De El Llano Del Reves' (prohibited area to bikes). This area is just before the 'km 13' road marker. On the far side of the road opposite this large lay-by there are two small singletrack paths descending away from the road. Take the lower one (GPS 1). Follow it first along a firebreak until you descend down the spine of a steep ridge. At the bottom of the ridge go to the left and continue winding down firebreaks towards the edge of the lake 'Embalse de Zahara - El Gastor'. Lots of gorse bushes make flat tyres commonplace. There are a variety of different ways to descend these slopes but you can clearly see where they go.

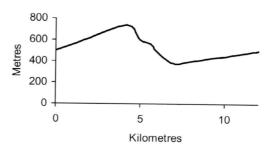

THE INACCESSIBLE PEAKS AND GORGES ARE
TEEMING WITH RARE WILDLIFE, PLANTS AND TREES.
CONSEQUENTLY THERE ARE FEW PLACES IN SPAIN
THAT ARE AS STRENUOUSLY PROTECTED

Ride 3: PR Route to Cortes de la Frontera

 30km

1 day

GPS points

N	W
1. **N36 44 391**	**W005 14 900**
2. **N36 43 219**	**W005 16 897**
3. **N36 40 915**	**W005 18 646**
4. **N36 44 684**	**W005 19 032**

Ride into Montejaque on the MA505 main road from the North. Just as you go downhill into town you pass a spring on the right (GPS 1). Turn right here onto a back road following signs to Refugio Cortijo de Libar and Bar La Cabana. After 700m turn right at the Las Yedras Bar. Go uphill leaving town on a concrete vehicle track south west into the hills. After 500m turn left at a fork onto a gravel vehicle track following GR/PR markers. After 3km the ascent ends at a handful of trees. Follow the main track to the left (GPS 2). You descend for a short while until the track levels out and you pass a farm on the right. 600m from the farm go through a gate. 3.5km further is a T-Junction (GPS 3) by the Refugio Cortijo de Libar. Turn left following a fence. After 700m the track you are on turns away from a fence on your left (GPS 4) then ends. Leave the track and follow the PR markers along the fence basically continuing straight up the centre of the valley directly away from the Refugio. The track becomes increasingly vague. You pass a farm. When the trail appears to end at a group of animal pens near the end of the valley go through an animal pen/corral to the left. It has metal discs like car hubcaps hanging from the fences and a large barbed wire-framed entrance. Go through this and clamber up the rocks towards a dip in between two peaks, heading for Cortes de la Frontera. Occasional yellow and white PR markers show the way. Half way up is a ruin and a house with solar panels a little further on. This PR path eventually becomes a superb descent that takes you into Cortes de la Frontera. You can either take the 19km road ride back to Montejaque or catch the train from Jimera to Benaojan, which leaves at about 5.30pm.

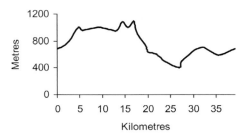

SIERRA DE GRAZALEMA RIDES

Ride 4: Singletrack above Zahara de la Sierra

↔ 19km

⧗ ½ day

GPS points

N	W
1. **N36 48 256**	*W005 23 383*
2. **N36 47 616**	*W005 22 942*
3. **N36 47 685**	*W005 22 904*

Follow the CA531 from the outskirts of Zahara. After 4.3km pass the start for ride 3 (GPS 1). About 2km further on the road you pass a concrete road marker 'km 15' marked on a concrete pillar on the side of the road. 700m from this point (about 7km from Zahara) you reach a small lay-by where there are four large concrete slabs on the right of the road. Although there are plenty of these protective blocks on the left of the road, this is the first group of four blocks on the right making them easy to find. From here a small singletrack descends below the road starting just after the last of these blocks (GPS 2). 240m downhill on this steep trail is a fork (GPS 3).

Ignore the right, which is an obvious track going uphill and take the far less obvious trail to the left. It becomes more defined the further you descend. NB there is a trail further uphill starting from the Puerto De Las Palomas.

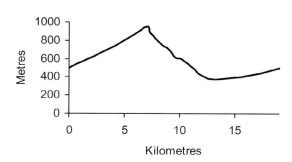

ACCOMMODATION

There are a lot of campsites but most are seasonal.
In winter they can open for holidays and the weekends.

Benamahoma
Camping Los Linares, Benamahoma, 956 716 275.

Grazalema
Camping Tajo Rodillo, Grazalema, 956 132 063.
Casa de Las Piedras, Grazalema, 956 132 014.
Villa Turística, Grazalema, 956 132 162.

Zahara de la Sierra
Camping Arroyomolinos, Zahara, 956 234 079.
Pensión Los Tadeos, Zahara, 956 123 086.
Hostal Marqués de Zahara, 956 123 061.
Hotel Arco de la villa, 956 12 32 30.

THE VILLAGES ARE OLD FORTRESS
TOWNS; DEFENSIBLE POSITIONS
REMNANTS OF ANCIENT
MOORISH STRONGHOLDS

Ride 5: The Camino El Bosque

↔ 17km

⏳ ½ day

GPS points

N	W
1. *N36 45 964*	*W005 28 184*

There is a ride along the side of the stream that runs between Benamahoma and El Bosque. From the centre of Benamahoma head out of town on the road downhill away from the campsite towards El Bosque. There is a steep hill at the bottom of which you come to the café Venta El Bujio opposite a furniture store. Turn right off the main road past the end of the café and bus shelter onto a small road that goes to a little bridge over a stream. Just before the little bridge is a left turn about 30m from the bus shelter. This slip road goes down to some green gates and a stream (GPS 1). Follow the sign post for Camino El Bosque, which is a singletrack along the left bank of the stream all the way to El Bosque. Be aware that this is a very popular walk and crowded with pedestrians in the weekend and summer months. Once you reach El Bosque either return the way you came or take the main road back to Benamahoma.

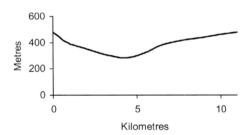

OTHER AREAS TO EXPLORE

The Serranía de Ronda Mountains also known as the Ronda valleys are very close and offer an abundance of trails. There is an annual race here that is called the "101 km in 24 hours". It is hosted by the 4th Spanish Legion Regiment and was originally designed for runners but a separate mountain bike event (longer than 101km) has developed. Visit www.ronda.net for details. It is held in mid-May and is spread over a whole weekend. The race for mountain-bikers is a 12-hour race. There is a big pasta festival for all competitors and it is well worth having a go.

Gaucín, The Parque Natural Sierra de las Nieves, El Chorro (all Málaga Province) and The Parque Natural de Alcornocarles (Cádiz Province) are also other worthy riding areas.

BALCÓN DE LA SERRANÍA

GAUCÍN
MÁLAGA - ANDALUCÍA

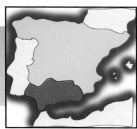

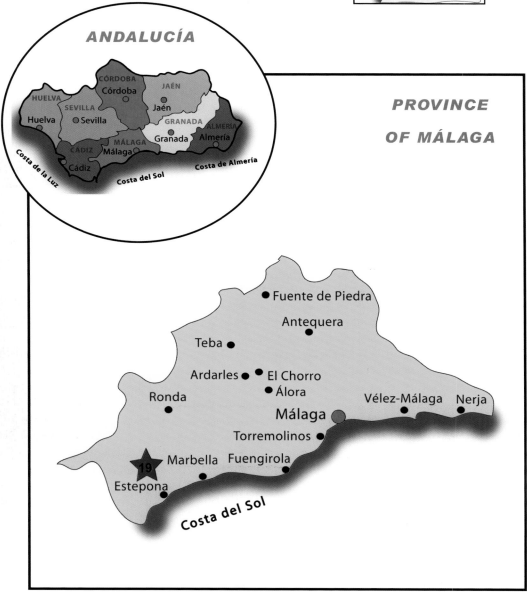

ANDALUCÍA

HUELVA
CÓRDOBA
Córdoba
JAÉN
Jaén
SEVILLA
Huelva
Sevilla
GRANADA
ALMERÍA
Granada
Almería
CÁDIZ
MÁLAGA
Málaga
Cádiz
Costa de la Luz
Costa del Sol
Costa de Almería

PROVINCE
OF MÁLAGA

Fuente de Piedra
Antequera
Teba
Ardarles
El Chorro
Álora
Ronda
Vélez-Málaga
Nerja
Málaga
Torremolinos
Marbella
Fuengirola
19
Estepona
Costa del Sol

GAUCÍN
SOUTHERN SPAIN

Location

Known locally as 'Gaucín Balcon de la Serranía' (the balcony of the mountains), the village has stunning vistas over the mouth of the Mediterranean. The hills drop in height away towards the sea leaving intense views of Estapona, Gibraltar and the African coast. Like most classic Andalucian villages, Gaucín is constructed like a cup cake; the white buildings frost the hill like icing and the cherry on top is provided by an obligatory Moorish castle. The town is just a stone's throw from the Costa Del Sol making it a destination providing both the delights of rural Spain as well as the comforts of the modern world.

General Background

There is an extremely well established international community in the town. These wealthy ex-pats have developed some luxurious local properties with the consequence that there is not an abundance of cheap places to stay. There is a slight undercurrent of tension between the locals and ex-pats. Being so close to major ports and the coast of Africa, there is a discernible presence of drugs. The town is known as a pueblo blanco, 'white village' not just because of its white walls! Due to the consistency of high winds, 'windmill' type turbines are being used along the spine road leading down to Estapona. A heated debate has begun. Simple graffiti reflects these entrenched positions. Some say 'molinos no!' (windmills - no) but this is often altered to '?molinos porque no?' (windmills - why not?); opinions are firmly divided.

The Weather

The moderate Mediterranean systems and more aggressive Atlantic weather combine over this high ground subjecting it to harsher conditions than the warmer seaside towns, such as Estapona, experience. Gaucín tends to attract cloudy, wet and windy conditions more readily than other Andalucian mountain villages that are further east. The winter months are slightly more protracted and strong winds are not uncommon.

Protected Status

There is little by way of restrictions to riding in this area. The farmers are fairly tolerant of you cutting across their land so long as you are respectful of their property.

Local Dangers

The wetter weather received allows a healthy growth of vegetation and a particularly common sight are the cork oak trees. These trees shed small, shiny leaves that behave like a sheet of ice when dry making it easy to loose traction. There are a wide variety of domestic and wild animals roaming the hills. Boars, bulls and pigs are all regularly encountered and they can all be quite aggressive in their own way. Treat all of them with respect.

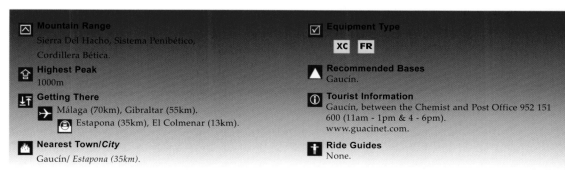

Mountain Range
Sierra Del Hacho, Sistema Penibético, Cordillera Bética.

Highest Peak
1000m

Getting There
✈ Málaga (70km), Gibraltar (55km).
Estapona (35km), El Colmenar (13km).

Nearest Town/City
Gaucín/ Estapona (35km).

Equipment Type
XC FR

Recommended Bases
Gaucín.

Tourist Information
Gaucín, between the Chemist and Post Office 952 151 600 (11am - 1pm & 4 - 6pm). www.guacinet.com.

Ride Guides
None.

WHITE BUILDINGS FROST THE
HILL LIKE ICING AND AN
OBLIGATORY MOORISH FORT
PROVIDES THE CHERRY ON TOP

PROS + CONS
+ Many English speaking locals
+ Rural retreat
+ Close to the coast
+ Long shaded vehicle tracks
− Expensive
− Hidden singletrack

☑ Equipment

Sharp, knobbly tyres cope better with the shiny cork oak leaves. Thin cross-country tyres can struggle for grip. Light, quick drying long sleeved tops can save you from serious lacerations to your forearms. The woodland floor can obviously create puncturing splinters making a good supply of inner tubes and puncture repair equipment useful.

XC FR Cross-Country and Freeride

Long vehicle track networks traverse the slopes of the wooded hillsides and cross country bikes are well suited to these conditions. It is best to meander through the woodland using these vehicle tracks to look for the elusive singletrack opportunities strewn about the hillsides. Trails created by wild animals are rewarding but often they are very narrow with tough undergrowth at all the wrong heights (i.e. level with face and groin). A slightly heavier free ride frame can be beneficial for pulling you through these dense sections of undergrowth.

DH Downhill

You will not thank yourself for bringing a heavy downhill bike here. Hunting for trails is an integral part of riding in Gaucín and doing this with a heavy bike can be horrendous in the heat.

👁 Local Observations

The riding in Gaucín is particularly attractive because of the woodland found there. The woods are on steep slopes littered with narrow singletrack created by wild and domestic animals that roam about. The drawbacks are the rapidly growing shrubs that make even regularly used trails become quickly overgrown. The riding here is therefore evolving all the time and all trails become impassable if not used regularly. Local riders are desperate for other riders to come and keep their routes in use so as to maintain them.

Although there are good shops for spares on the coast, there is very little in Gaucín so being well supplied is important if you don't want to spend time travelling to the coast.

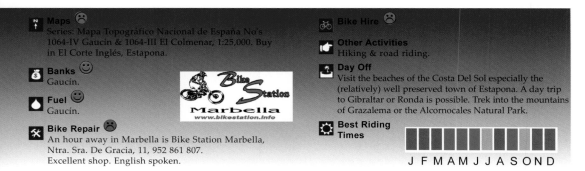

Maps 😞
Series: Mapa Topográfico Nacional de España No's 1064-IV Gaucín & 1064-III El Colmenar, 1:25,000. Buy in El Corte Inglés, Estapona.

Banks 🙂
Gaucin.

Fuel 🙂
Gaucin.

Bike Repair 😞
An hour away in Marbella is Bike Station Marbella, Ntra. Sra. De Gracia, 11, 952 861 807. Excellent shop. English spoken.

Bike Hire 😞

Other Activities 👍
Hiking & road riding.

Day Off
Visit the beaches of the Costa Del Sol especially the (relatively) well preserved town of Estapona. A day trip to Gibraltar or Ronda is possible. Trek into the mountains of Grazalema or the Alcornocales Natural Park.

Best Riding Times

J F M A M J J A S O N D

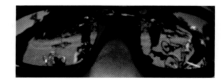

GAUCIN RIDES

Ride 1: La Claria

↔ 4.5km

⧗ ¼ day

▼ ▪

◔ ▪

⬚ ☹

GPS points

N	W
1. N36 31 195	W005 19 510

Start facing the petrol station (GPS 1) with Gaucin behind you and you will see a small road running up the right hand side of the petrol station. Take this. Tarmac quickly turns to dusty vehicle track. After 1.16km pass a green corrugated roofed farm building. A few hundred metres further and you reach a farm house 'La Claria'. Go through the gateposts. At the first fork after the farm go uphill i.e. left. Go through a gate that is a fence gate. Keep climbing to a second gate. Keep climbing. Eventually you come to the foot of the peak of the mountain where there is another crude fence gate, after which there is a choice of three paths: left, right or straight on. Go left descending back to the main road.

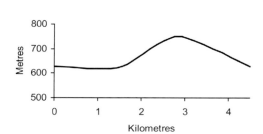

Ride 2: Short Town Circuit

↔ 7km

⧗ 2 hours

▼ ▪

◔ ▪

⬚ ☺

GPS points

N	W
1. N36 31 195	W005 19 510
2. N36 32 177	W005 18 107
1. N36 32 271	W005 18 171
1. N36 32 283	W005 18 175
1. N36 31 523	W005 18 774

Turn left out of Gaucín's main petrol station (GPS 1) on the CA369 road (towards Ronda). After 3.3km turn left into a lay-by signed 'Gaucín Balcón de la Serranía'. Go through gates marked 'Ano 1981' (GPS 2) and follow the vehicle track. Ignore the first left after about 30m. After 250m from the road you pass a spring/fuente on the right (GPS 3). Take the left turn opposite this (GPS 4). This vehicle track becomes very technical single track and arrives back at the town at (GPS 5).

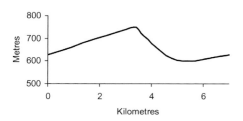

THE HILLS DROP AWAY TOWARDS
THE SEA LEAVING INTENSE VIEWS
OF ESTAPONA, GIBRALTAR AND
THE AFRICAN COAST

Ride 3: Balcón de la Serranía Singletrack

↔ **11km**

⧗ **¼ day**

🍸 ▮

💧 ▮

▣ ☹

GPS points

N	W
1. *N36 31 195*	*W005 19 510*
2. *N36 31 778*	*W005 19 709*
3. *N36 32 441*	*W005 20 030*
4. *N36 32 222*	*W005 20 216*
5. *N36 32 416*	*W005 19 5917*

Start facing the petrol station (GPS 1) and take the small road running up the right hand side of it. The road soon becomes a vehicle track. After 1.16km pass a large green corrugated roofed farm building on your right. 240m past this (GPS 2) take the tiny singletrack decent to your right that is barely a tyre's width across. (It is hard to spot. It begins 30m before a left-hand bend in the track just around which is a farm called 'La Claria'). Descend for a few hundred metres to a T-junction. Turn right. Cross a vehicle track. Follow the trail along a fence on your left for 50m to a crude gate in the fence. Go through it. Descend on singletrack until it meets a vehicle track. Go left for a few hundred metres until you pass a stack of large, distinct boulders on the left. 85m from here is a grassy spur on the right where the singletrack descent continues (GPS 3). It ends at a large gate at the bottom of the valley. Ascend on the vehicle track without going through the gate. Ignore the first right turn that goes to a farm. Climb to a T-junction (GPS 4) Go left downhill. After a short descent take the first chained vehicle track on the right (GPS 5). Climb back up until the track is blocked by a fence/gate. Go through this and continue climbing until you return to the green corrugated roofed building at the start of the ride. Head left here back into town.

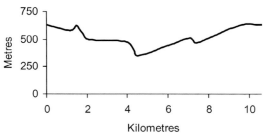

GAUCIN RIDES

Ride 4: Chapel of Juan de Dios

↔ **7km**

⧖ **¼ day**

🍴 ▪

💧 ▪

⬚ ☺

GPS points

N	W
1. **N36 31 195**	**W005 19 510**
2. **N36 31 380**	**W005 18 916**
3. **N36 31 233**	**W005 18 949**

From Gaucín's petrol station on the CA369 (GPS 1) turn left on the main road heading up the valley towards Ronda. After 1.2km take the last turning on the right into Gaucín (GPS 2) and go over a couple of speed bumps for 240m until you reach house number 76 on Queipo de Llano. Turn left onto a brick road then left again onto a concrete track after only 30m (GPS 3). Descend steeply. After 600m go right at a fork. Pass a blockish building. Singletrack begins after an old farm. It comes to an end at a vehicle track. Turn right onto this and immediately you come to a 3-way junction with a thin cypress fir tree facing you. Go right steeply uphill. Take the first left passing through large reddish/brown gates. The trail dips down then up and passes under power cables. Before the track descends again, go sharp right and climb up to a T-junction in front of a pylon. Go left downhill until you pass a keg-shaped Ermita - Chapel of Juan de Dios. Follow the trail past this. Pass sandy coloured modern houses on left just after which you meet a more pronounced track. Go left uphill. When the main road appears beneath you, ignore the main track that drops down to the road. Turn right and climb up and away from the road. Follow this tough climb on an old cobbled Roman road back to Gaucín.

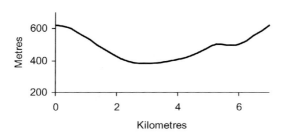

Ride 5: Balcón de la Serrania

↔ 20km

⧗ ½ day

🍸 ▪

🍶 ▪

▣ ☺

GPS points

N	W
1. N36 31 195	W005 19 510
2. N36 32 177	W005 18 107
3. N36 33 083	W005 18 949
4. N36 32 222	W005 20 216
5. N36 31 858	W005 20 914
6. N36 31 760	W005 21 435

Turn left out of Gaucín's petrol station (GPS 1) on the CA369 road and descend, heading in the direction of Ronda. The road starts to ascend as you pass the last buildings of the town. 3.4km from the petrol station turn left into a lay-by with the sign 'Gaucín Balcón de la Serranía'. Go through the gates (GPS 2) and follow the main vehicle track passing a spring on the right almost immediately. 4km from the gates a vehicle track joins from the left. Turn left. After 550m there is a fork, go right downhill. Descend steeply for 665m through a few 180° bends until the gradient lessens and a grassy area opens up on the left (GPS 3). Join the (initially obscure) singletrack descent on the left. Follow it for about 1km until it rejoins the vehicle track lower down. Descend to the river and cross it. Follow the vehicle track on the far side for a few hundred metres to the first T-junction and turn left. A long ascent follows. Ignore the first right turn to a farm (2.2km from river). After about 3km of climbing turn right at the first T-junction you come to (GPS 4). Ascend for 1.85km passing Cortijo El Peso (GPS 5). 1km from here you reach the MA512 road (GPS 6). Go left for 2.3km until you rejoin the MA369. Turn left and follow this for 1.3km back to Gaucín.

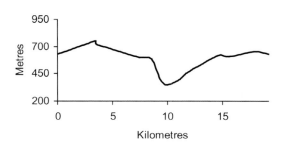

PLANT GROWTH IS PROLIFIC AND
TRAILS BECOME IMPASSABLE IF NOT
USED REGULARLY. LOCAL RIDERS ARE
KEEN FOR OTHERS TO USE THEM

GAUCIN RIDES

Ride 6: Smuggler's Route

↔ **16km**

⏳ **½ day**

GPS points

N	W
1. N36 31 195	W005 19 510
2. N36 30 784	W005 20 946
3. N36 30 739	W005 20 947

From petrol station (GPS 1) Head out of Gaucín on the CA369 main road to Algeceris. After 2.2km pass the MA512 turning to Colmenar on the right. ignore this and continue on the road for 640m then turn onto the first vehicle track on your left (GPS 2). Immediately there is a fork. Turn right. On your right is a small ditch. After about 60 metres there is a blockish stone about ½ metre x ¼ metre where a tiny singletrack begins traversing the ridge on your right (GPS 3). Ascend this until it climbs up and over the ridge. Follow the singletrack until it eventually rejoins a vehicle track where you can either go right to rejoin the main road or go left all the way down to the river. Use the road to return to Gaucín.

ACCOMMODATION

There is not an abundance of cheap places to stay in the area and there is no campsite. The closest one is found on the CA 369 main road at Algatocín as you head towards Ronda.

Gaucín
La, Almuña, Apartado 20, 29480, Gaucín, 952 151 200.
Hotel Casablanca, Calle Teodoro de Molina 12, 29480, Gaucín, 952 151 019.

Casares
Pensíon Plaza, Plaza de España 6, 952 894 088.

Estepona
Hostal El Pilar, Plaza Las Flores 22, 952 800 018.
Hotel Buenavista, Paseo Marítimo 180, 952 800 137.

BOARS, BULLS AND PIGS ARE
ALL REGULARLY ENCOUNTERED
AND CAN BE AGGRESSIVE,
TREAT THEM WITH RESPECT!

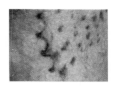

OTHER AREAS TO EXPLORE

There are countless wooded hills in these parts. The
Serrania de Ronda are between here and Ronda and
host the 24 hour race 'The Ronda 101km Challenge'.
It is worth visiting Casares, El Colmenar, the
Parque Natural de Grazalema, Parque Natural de
Alcornocales and around Barbate (Parque Natural
La Breña y Marismas Del Barbate)

ALCORNOCALES NATURAL PARK

ALCORNOCALES NATURAL PARK

CÁDIZ - ANDALUCÍA

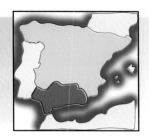

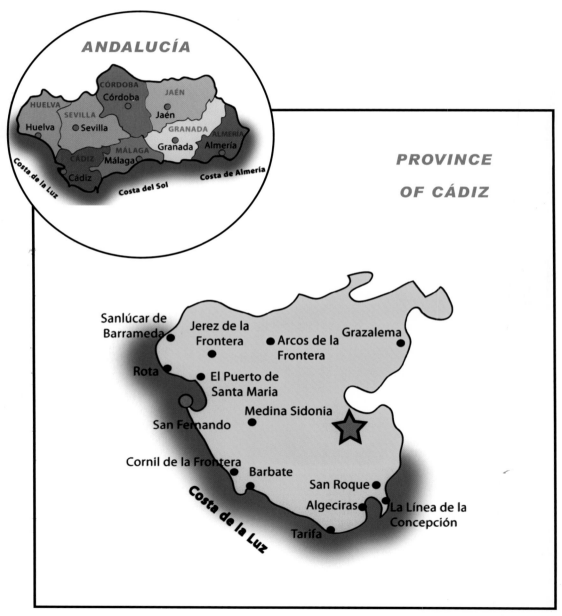

ANDALUCÍA

HUELVA
Huelva

CÓRDOBA
Córdoba

SEVILLA
Sevilla

JAÉN
Jaén

GRANADA
Granada

ALMERÍA
Almería

MÁLAGA
Málaga

CÁDIZ
Cádiz

Costa de la Luz

Costa del Sol

Costa de Almería

PROVINCE
OF CÁDIZ

Sanlúcar de
Barrameda

Jerez de la
Frontera

Arcos de la
Frontera

Grazalema

Rota

El Puerto de
Santa Maria

San Fernando

Medina Sidonia

Cornil de la Frontera

Barbate

San Roque

Algeciras

La Línea de la
Concepción

Tarifa

Costa de la Luz

ALCORNOCALES

SOUTHERN SPAIN

Location

The Los Alcornocales Natural Park is a huge expanse of forest (170,000 Hectares) located between Tarifa in the south and Grazalema Natural Park in the north.

General Background

It is the largest preserved oak woodland in Europe with cork oaks being the dominant tree and from where the park gets its name.

The Weather

Mediterranean and Atlantic weather systems mix creating a humid climate. Rainfall is high due to westerly Atlantic winds. In spring and summer the wet and warm 'Levante' wind from North Africa keeps the area humid creating thick morning and evening mists.

Protected Status

Riding on footpaths is prohibited because it is dangerous due to a combination of factors: hunters with powerful rifles, paths that are dangerous to travel in after downpours and major repair works being carried out from time to time. Consequently you must check with the Tourist Office or Environment Office in Alcalá de Las Gazules to see where you can ride and you may be required to carry a pass issued by these offices. They are free.

Equipment

Rainfall can be heavy so carry a waterproof. Tyres with traction are needed for the year round slippery conditions. They need to be good at clearing mud. Good supplies of tubes essential.

Cross-Country

Only vehicle track riding is permissible so this is a cross-country venue only.

Local Observations

The humid, sub-tropical climate supports a variety of unusual plant-life The result is a verdant landscape of trees covered in mosses, tendrils of plants hanging in the mist creating a distinctly fairyland feel. There is little light pollution so the area is great for stargazing. Visit the attractive town of Jimena de la Frontera.

The park is beautiful, unusual and therefore heavily protected by local authorities. Although no singletrack riding is permitted, the area is worthy of mention because it is an incredibly attractive forest with technical vehicle tracks passing through steep valleys. The scenery you pass - moss covered gnarly old oaks and sub-tropical vegetation - enhances the rides.

Mountain Range
Cordillera Bética.

Highest Peak
1091m.

Getting There
Cádiz (75km), Málaga (170km).
Algeciras (50km).

Nearest Town/City
Alcalá de Los Gazules/*Algeciras (50km)*.

Equipment Type
XC

Recommended Bases
Alcalá de Los Gazules.

Tourist Information
Oficina Parque Natural Los Alcornocales, Pza San Jorge, Alcalá de Los Gazules, 956 413 307.
Ceder Parque Natural De Los Alcornocales, Alcalá de Los Gazules, 956 413 813, www.alcornocales.org.

Other Activities
Rock climbing, ornithology, botany, hunting, hiking, canoeing, potholing, fishing.

TENDRILS OF PLANTS
HANGING IN THE MIST
CREATE A DISTINCTLY
FAIRYLAND FEEL

PROS + CONS

\+ Isolated riding in rare environs
\+ A wild, wooded wilderness

\- Remote
\- No singletrack

RIDES

The tourist offices in Alcalá de Los Gazules has mapped bike routes for the following:
1.Picacho - Peguera (Alcalá de Los Gazules)
2.La Sauceda (Cortes De la Frontera)
3.Berrueco - Cañillas (Near Cortes de la Frontera)
4.Puerto Del Bujeo (Near Tarifa)
5.Carbrito - Bujeo (Near Tarifa)

Ride 1: La Sauceda

↔ **20 km**

⧗ **½ day**

🍴 ◼

🛢 ◼

▣ ☺

This ride starts at La Sauceda Area Recreativa, which is found mid-way on the main road between Alcalá de Los Gazules and Jimena de la Frontera (at the km 34 road marker). There is a large sundial and an office for the forest authorities opposite a parking area. The circuit starts opposite the parking area. Go through a green gate to the left. Stay on this track for the entire circuit. You end by descending in front of the Forestry building.

Ride 2: Picacho - Peguera

↔ **42 km**

⧗ **1 day**

🍴 ◼

🛢 ◼

▣ ☺

There is a 42.5 km forest track ride going from the Refugio Del Picacho and the Arroyo de la Peguera. It starts near Alcalá de Los Gazules at km 68.5 on the Puerto de Gális to Alcalá de Los Gazules Road. 3.5km from the start you pass the Refugio Del Picacho. Following a north-south direction, the track traverses the western slopes of Picacho, Aljibe & Montero Mountains. You cross the Arroyos/streams called Puerto Oscuro, Montero, Alberite, Laurel, Arnao and Peguera. After about 20km you pass the Refugio Barrancones.

Maps ☺
Mapa Topográfico Nacional de España, Jimena de la Frontera 1071 - I
Mapa Topográfico Nacional de España, Alcalá de Los Gazules 1070 - I & II.

Banks ☺
Alcalá de Los Gazules.

Fuel ☹
Alcalá de Los Gazules.

Bike Repair ☹

Bike Hire ☹

Day Off
Eating in the hunting lodge type restaurants found in the park. Take a day trip to Gibraltar. Go to the beaches on the Costa de la Luz. Visit the castle in Jimena de la Frontera.

Best Riding Times

J F M A M J J A S O N D

LA BREÑA Y MARISMAS DEL BARBATE NATURAL PARK

LA BREÑA Y MARISMAS DEL BARBATE NATURAL PARK
CÁDIZ - ANDALUCÍA

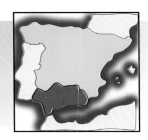

ANDALUCÍA

PROVINCE OF CÁDIZ

BARBATE
SOUTHERN SPAIN

 Location

The 'La Breña y Marismas Del Barbate Natural Park' is located on the Costa de la Luz mid way between Cádiz and Tarifa. It is the smallest Natural Park in Spain at just 9,382 acres and it is based on an ancient sand dune system colonised by a great mass of pine trees and rare plants. The Costa Trafalga is the stretch of coves and beaches encompassing Barbate, Zahara de los Atunes, Los Caños de Meca and Zahora.

General Background

This windy and unspoilt part of the coast has remnants of castles and towers used to warn the locals of imminent pirate attacks. These proved useless in 1805 when Nelson's fleet caught the Spanish unawares and decimated their navy. Cabo Trafalgar (Trafalgar Cove) was named in honour of the event. The Roman ruins of Baelo Claudio near Bolonia have a fish factory and this is still the main industry in the area. The town of Barbate is based around a port and a declining canning industry making it a fairly uninspiring place to stay. Base yourself at Los Caños de Meca an old hippy hideaway with a very chilled summer fiesta vibe, Zahara de los Atunes, or Tarifa and make a day trip to this part of the coast. The trade in illegal immigrants and drugs from Africa is very evident in this part of Spain. The news often has results of drugs busts or discoveries of bodies on the beach of those who did not survive the treacherous crossing.

The Weather

The park is at the mouth of the Mediterranean on the south western coast of Spain so it is subject to Atlantic weather systems. This means it is distinctly different to the Mediterranean weather at the nearby Costa Del Sol. Winds are stronger and temperatures a little cooler.

Protected Status

Natural Park regulations apply.

Mountain Range
N/A.

Highest Peak
Meca (169m).

Getting There
✈ Cádiz (56km), Málaga (200km).
🚌 Cádiz (56km).

Nearest Town/City
Barbate/*Cádiz (56km)*.

Equipment Type
XC

Recommended Bases
Caños de Meca, Zahara de los Atunes, Tarifa.

Tourist Information
Barbate Tourist Office, 956 433 962.
turismo@aytobarbate.org
www.barbate.net.

Ride Guides
Terra Explora, Barbate, 956 431 505.

THE BULK OF THE RIDING HERE IS ON DRY, FAST, GRITTY TRACKS, CUTTING THROUGH THE PINEWOODS

PROS + CONS
+ Chill-out seaside spot
+ Wind swept beaches

- Limited riding
- Major illicit drugs trade

☠ Local Dangers

Associated with the organised criminal activity comes bandit style break-ins to cars so be aware of your valuables. Don't let this put you off a visit. There is a bohemian feel in the air with a vibrant youth culture. Talented graffiti artists, skilful bikers and competent board riders abound. Behave sensibly, park safely and enjoy.

☑ Equipment

The terrain is sandy, dusty and dry so you will need lots of lube. There are no major descents or ascents so light fast bikes are best. Semi-slick tyres will suffice.

XC Cross-Country

With the highest hill in the area under 200m there is little challenging riding.

👁 Local Observations

Sand may cause your bike grief. This is one place where a cheap bike that you don't mind getting gritty will do. On the plus side, all this sand has created the endless idyllic golden stretches of beaches. A very straight road running between Barbate and Caños de Meca cuts through the pinewoods that contain the bulk of the riding. The beauty of riding in this area is the fact that you can enjoy tame but agreeable rides whilst enjoying a relaxed, unhurried beach holiday; you are never far from a seaside bar, restaurant or club. There is usually a cooling sea breeze that can keep you active even in the summer heat.

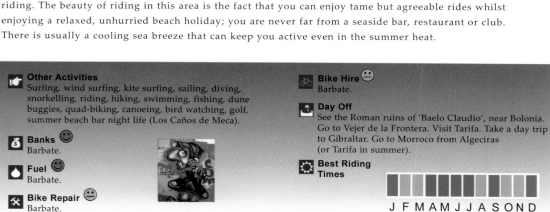

Other Activities
Surfing, wind surfing, kite surfing, sailing, diving, snorkelling, riding, hiking, swimming, fishing, dune buggies, quad-biking, canoeing, bird watching, golf, summer beach bar night life (Los Caños de Meca).

Banks 🙂
Barbate.

Fuel 🙂
Barbate.

Bike Repair 😐
Barbate.

Bike Hire 😐
Barbate.

Day Off
See the Roman ruins of 'Baelo Claudio', near Bolonia. Go to Vejer de la Frontera. Visit Tarifa. Take a day trip to Gibraltar. Go to Morroco from Algeciras (or Tarifa in summer).

Best Riding Times

J F M A M J J A S O N D

BARBATE RIDES

Generalised maps are available from the tourist office in barbate outlining 2 mountain bike routes which explore the Costa Trafalgar. One encirlces the Barbate marsh area and the other takes in the marshes and the surrounding pine woodland. Neither are taxing due to the lack of contours in this area but make sure you take lots of water as there are very few springs en route.

Ride 1: El Rancho Grande

⬌ 15km

⌛ ½ day

Head from Barbate on the A 393 main road to Vejer de la Frontera. At various places on either side of the road there are singletrack paths to keep you off the busy road. After a few kilometres on your left you will see a white wall that is signed Rancho Grande. Turn left off the road onto the sand track going through the wall. Follow the track past the ranch up hill until you begin to pass through farmland. A wind farm is visible in the distance on your right. At the first major T-junction turn left away from the wind turbines. Descend into a dip and climb out the other side passing a large house at the top. Eventually you cross a cattle grid and enter the pinewoods. Take the first major left after the cattle grid and a sandy track takes you back to Barbate.

ALTHOUGH A SUMMER PARTY
VIBE PREVAILS, BARBATE IS A
SUPRISINGLY UNSPOILT AND
IDYLLIC STRETCH OF COASTLINE

ACCOMMODATION

Caños de Meca
Hostal Los Castillejos, 956 437 019.
Hostal Villa Guadalupe, 956 437 220.
Mar y Sol, 956 437 255.
Camping Caños de Meca, 956 437 120.

Zahara de los Atunes
Hostal Monte Mar, 956 439 047.
Hotel Gran Sol, 956 439 301.
Hostal Castro, 956 439 358.

El Palmar
Hosstal Francisco, 956 232 788.
Hostal La Ilusión, 956 232 398.
Camping El Palmar, 956 232 161.